MW01440234

Cover and book design: Daniele Zizzi

Codice ISBN: 9798313563213

Conclave: the rules for electing the next Pope

Updated with the latest changes

Javier Martínez-Brocal
Fr. José de Jesús Aguilar

INDEX

Introduction

It is fascinating how throughout history the rules of the conclave have evolved to guarantee the freedom of the electors and of whoever is elected pope.

The mechanism, precise as a Swiss watch, is set in motion at the exact moment when the resignation of the bishop of Rome takes effect or his death is announced. From that moment on, the Vatican machinery is guided by a specific law that indicates who is in charge and the limits of his authority, establishes the protocol for paying homage to the deceased pope and specifies the terms for finding a new successor to the apostle Peter.

During this period, the "Sede Vacante", or the vacancy of the Holy See as it is called, the Vatican expresses mourning and openness to the future through gestures of great significance dating back to the first millennium. Deciphering them allows us to understand the richness of this institution and the weight that will be assumed by whoever becomes the new pontiff in the conclave.

*

One of the first lessons I received as a "vaticanista",

which is the name given in Italy to journalists who try to decipher the gestures and words of the popes, has to do precisely with the conclave.

When I landed in Rome in September 2003 to begin a new professional adventure as a reporter, the first assignment I received was to prepare the coverage of the conclave, which was considered "imminent". At the time, John Paul II was celebrating the 25th anniversary of his election, and he could no longer articulate words in his public meetings. At each audience, one of his collaborators would read the speech on his behalf and he would appear stiffly and impart a blessing with great difficulty.

I remember that during those months I studied attentively both the hidden meanings in the ritual linked to the last days of a pope and the mechanism for electing his successor. I came into contact with the history of the conclaves, the legends about each papal election, the old movie images of the voting. I studied the lists of "papabile", as media calls the main candidates to papacy, memorized the names and surnames of all the cardinals, scrutinized their interviews in search of clues about their intentions for the future of the Church.

I believe that thanks to this "excess of information", when "la emergenza" ("the emergency") arrived, a coded expression used by the Italian press to refer to the future death of the pontiff and the election of his successor, I was able to be attentive and recount in my chronicles what was unexpected, what really made those days a unique event.

From those days in April 2005, I remember, for example, that during the last hours of John Paul II, tens of thousands of Romans gathered spontaneously under his window in St. Peter's Square to accompany him physically. I remember that I was able to enter the pope's first wake, in the Sala Clementina, a few hours after his death, and recognize the elements that ancient Roman law and ancestral Roman custom have set in place to honor the pontiff's remains. I was in the Sistine Chapel and saw up close the seats of the cardinal electors, and the two "stoves" that would produce the smoke with which they would give an account of the result.

At that conclave I met the Mexican priest and great communicator Fr. José de Jesús Aguilar. We worked together in the coverage for Televisión Azteca of Mexico and I was impressed by his ability to provide quality content in those long live broadcasts. I greatly appreciated his ability to explain with precision and very good humor complex concepts related to the Catholic Church, the life of the Pope, Vatican protocol or Christian symbols in great works of art.

Hours of work together led to a friendship and gave me the opportunity to collaborate with him. Moreover, Aguilar returned to Rome for many other Vatican coverage events, such as the beatification of John Paul II in May 2011, the resignation of Benedict XVI and the conclave that elected Pope Francis.

I will not forget that on March 13, 2013, we had lunch together to prepare for the afternoon telecast, convinced that on that very day we would have "fumata bianca", "white smoke", and meet the new pope. Over a plate of "spaghetti alle vongole", spaghetti with clams, we reviewed together the rules of the conclave and the rich ritual that is followed in the Sistine Chapel when someone gets more than two-thirds of the votes. We also looked to the future of the Catholic Church and with it in mind we tried to imagine the name the new pope would adopt. "There are some who are asking for his name to be Francis, like the patron saint of Italy, a name that no pontiff has ever had," I told him. Javier Alatorre, the channel's star presenter, from whom I have also learned a lot, was listening to us. "What if the new pope were named Francis?" he immediately posted on social networks. He got it right.

More than ten years have passed since that election, during which time there have been many important changes in the ritual and norms that govern the Vatican and the Catholic Church during this delicate period called the "Sede Vacante".

One morning in the year 2023, while we were walking through the Basilica of St. Paul Outside the Walls very close to the Tiber, on the Via Ostiense, next to the tomb of that Saul who fell from his horse on the road to Damascus, Father José de Jesús proposed that I update his book "Sede Vacante". "A lot has happened since I wrote it, why don't you revise it and add all the updates?".

The idea was to respect the original structure and the very useful scheme of questions and answers. I undertook the task thinking that it would be finished in one or two weeks. However, as I progressed, new questions arose that supplemented the answers: Benedict XVI's resignation brought about changes in protocol, in customs and also in norms. Benedict had twice modified the law on the conclave, and Francis also modified some fundamental aspects of the funeral ritual of the popes and the distribution of power and functions during the Vacancy of the Holy See

"Father, I've come up with a lot of topics. More than supplementing, the result is a new book," I told him with some fear. "What good news!" he replied. "It is going to help many people now and in the future to know the keys to the Church, to understand how the way to elect the Pope has evolved and to look at what is important when they have to follow this story," he answered me enthusiastically.

The result is this work. Sometimes the starting point is the answer in the original edition, but I have always tried to add new information to help understand the issue being addressed. There are many new questions and I have avoided others so as not to stray from the main topic.

Naturally, the successes are attributable to Father José de Jesús. As for the mistakes, I personally assume the blame.

I'd like to thank Claire Ptaschinski for reviewing - and improving a lot! - the English version.

Javier Martínez-Brocal
Rome, March 5, 2025

Vatican.
A bit of History and Geography

Why does the pope live in Rome and not in Jerusalem, Nazareth or Bethlehem, the land of Jesus?

The pope is the successor of the apostle Peter, who was the first bishop of Rome and died a martyr's death there. The pope's mission is linked to his role as successor to St. Peter, the apostle who received the mandate from Jesus to be the "Rock" on which the Church was to be built. Therefore, the heart of Christianity is not linked to the place where this religion was born, but to the mission entrusted to Peter.

The truth is that Christianity had a very reduced presence in Jerusalem. Already a few years after the Resurrection of Jesus, even in the time of the apostles, many Christians had to flee that city because of the hostility of the religious authorities of the Temple of Jerusalem. Later, in 70 A.D., Jerusalem was destroyed by the Roman Empire and both Jews and Christians had to flee from there.

Where does the name Vatican come from?

The territory west of the Tiber River that makes up the current Vatican City was known in ancient times as *Ager Vaticanus* ("*Vatican Fields*"). According to some historians, the name derives from the Latin "*vates*", "fortune-teller", because in ancient Rome, before the arrival of Christianity, soothsayers and magicians performed omens or predictions on that hill. Others believe that the name evokes the name of its first inhabitants, who belonged to an ancient Etruscan settlement called *Vaticum*.

At what point does the Vatican become an important place for Christians?

It becomes an important place for Christians when Peter is buried in the necropolis that was in that place.

Around the year 40 A.D. Caligula began the construction of a circus in the Vatican area for chariot races, which was completed by his nephew Nero. The place was imposing and had a capacity for about 20,000 spectators. The emperor's delusions led him to torture people in his shows, for example, by burning them alive to bring light to the area.

The Christians did not escape this tragedy. In the year 64 or 67 A.D., between 200 and 300 were martyred there, among them St. Peter, who was probably crucified. His disciples buried him in the nearby necropolis and from that moment the Vatican was forever linked to the history of Christianity and became a pilgrimage destination.

In the time of the apostle Peter, this place was outside Rome. Decades later, between 134 and 139, the emperor Hadrian built the *Pons Aelius* or "Elius Bridge" to communicate the city with his mausoleum, the current Castel Sant'Angelo. Thus, the Vatican area was linked to the city of Rome.

In the 4th century, once the persecution of the followers of Jesus was over, the emperor Constantine began to build a Christian basilica over the tomb of the apostle Peter. The pontiffs of the Middle Ages bought the surrounding territory and built a residence

Is the Vatican currently a neighborhood of Rome?

Those who visit Rome also refer to the Vatican as an area of the Eternal City, even though politically it is not so. Although it is encompassed by the Borgo district, it is treated as a country separate from Italy, called the Vatican City State. It has its own regime, its own law, flag, anthem and borders. Some of its border crossings are the St. Anne's Gate, the Perugino Gate or the Holy Office Gate.

When did the Vatican become an independent, free and sovereign state?

The present configuration of the Vatican City State dates back to 1929. Its sovereignty and international juridical identity were recognized on February 11 of that year with the Lateran Treaty, signed between the Holy See and the Kingdom of Italy. The new state, born almost 60 years after the fall of the Papal States, was constituted as an entity distinct from the Holy See. The latter is the governing body of the Catholic Church, and the Vatican City State is the physical territory over which civil government is exercised.

How big is the territory of the Vatican City State?

It is 44 hectares and is the smallest country in the world. Its territory includes the Basilica and St. Peter's Square, the Apostolic Palace, with the famous Sistine Chapel, the Vatican museums and gardens, as well as a treasured library containing works that are part of humanity's cultural heritage. Another of the treasures inside the Vatican are its historical archives containing records of the presence of the Church and its relationship with the world.

How did the Vatican become a country and the pope a head of state?

With the progressive fall of the Western Roman Empire, there was a power vacuum in the Italian peninsula, which from the 6th century onwards, in practice, was filled by the pope, since he was the only authority stably recognized by the population. Thus, in the 8th century, the Papal State emerged and quickly dominated the territories that today correspond to central and northern Italy.

The pontiff was interested in assuming temporal power in a geographical territory because he feared that, without a territory of its own, the Church would be at the mercy of the will of the emperors. The idea was to protect its independence and freedom.

Has the Pope always lived in the Vatican?

No. The area of the Vatican was uninhabited for many centuries, as it was a swampy area on the other side of the bank of the Tiber River, outside the city of Rome. Then, the pope's residence was in Rome, in the area of the Cathedral of St. John Lateran.

Political and religious problems often forced the pontiff to escape from Rome and move his residence to other Italian cities such as Anagni, Orvieto and Viterbo, and even in the twelfth century several popes resided in the French city of Avignon. When they returned to Rome from France in 1377, they found the rooms of St. John Lateran so dilapidated that they decided to build a new residence on the Vatican grounds, next to St. Peter's Basilica. The new complex would include the pontiff's rooms and his private chapel, the Sistine Chapel. To build and embellish it, a few centuries later, artists such as Botticelli, Perugino, Fra Angelico, Bramante, Raphael, Michelangelo and Bernini were set to work.

During what period did the pontiffs live in Avignon (France)?

The pontiffs resided in Avignon, France, during the period from 1309 to 1377. The move was made by Pope Clement V, under pressure from King Philip IV of France. At first the decision was only provisional. At that time the city belonged to vassals of the pope, and later, in 1348, it became papal property. The seven popes of this period were all French, as were 111 of the 134 cardinals appointed during that period.

Why did the papacy move to Avignon?

At the end of the 11th century, both the Papal States and the city of Rome were politically paralyzed by pressures from European monarchs and rival families, due to problems related to territory, administration or privileges, which the pontiffs had not always dealt with fairly. These tensions had created delicate situations, such as the resignation of Pope Celestine V, the conspiracy against Boniface VIII, or the flight from Rome to Perugia of Benedict XI in 1304 due to threats from the powerful Colonna family - where, in fact, he died a few months later.

In Perugia, after eleven months of disputes between cardinals for and against the political decisions of the last two pontiffs, Boniface VIII and Benedict XI, on June 5, 1305, the bishop of Bordeaux (France), Bertrand de Got, was elected pope, since he was not on either side and had remained neutral.

The new pope, who was called Clement V, was always subject to the influence of the French monarch Philip the Fair, who proposed that he move to Avignon, at that time a papal territory attached to France. Clement accepted because, in addition to the threats that awaited him in Rome, he wanted to unite the forces of France and England to launch a crusade in the Holy Land. Thus, Clement went to reside in Avignon, although without the intention of transferring the Holy See there.

His first successor, John XXII, also reaffirmed the "provisional" decision to stay in Avignon. However, no pope returned to Rome until 1369. Urban V did, but he was in the Urbe for only one year. Urban returned to Avignon because he found the Eternal City in ruins and ungovernable due to the struggles between noble families and did not receive the expected support from the Germanic emperor.

The clamor of Catholics for the return of Peter's successor to Rome grew over the years and was such that Cardinal Pierre Roger de Beaufort promised to

God in secret that he would do just that if he became pontiff. When he was elected pope in 1370 and became Gregory XI, it took another prodigious event for him to fulfill that promise. He returned definitively to Rome in 1377.

Thus, the papacy was out of Rome for 67 years. In Avignon, the Papal Palaces are preserved, as well as the cathedral, where the image of the Virgin of Our Lady of All Power is venerated. Some popes are also buried there.

Which pope bought the city of Avignon?

In 1348 Pope Clement VI bought the sovereignty over the city of Avignon from Queen Joan I of Naples and Provence for 80,000 gold florins. At that point, the city became part of the Papal States.

What prodigious sign did the pope receive to return to Rome?

When he was a cardinal, the future Pope Gregory XI, secretly made a promise to God to return the papacy to Rome. He did it without mentioning it to anyone, neither before, nor after. But in an apparition, Jesus revealed this promise to St. Catherine of Siena, and she presented herself before the pontiff to ask him for an account and to urge him to fulfill it. As a result, Gregory left Avignon in 1376 and entered Rome on January 17, 1377. These were not easy times. At the end of May, he was forced to flee and take refuge in Anagni because of a popular revolt. He returned definitively to Rome on November 7 of the same year and died there in 1378.

What happened in Avignon when the pope left for Rome?

With the death of Gregory XI, in 1378 a new pope was elected in Rome without waiting for the French cardinals, for fear that the elected one would return to Avignon. Therefore, when they found out, they considered the election of Urban VI illegitimate and elected Clement VII as "antipope". This resulted in the "Western Schism".

From 1378 until 1417, for 39 years, there was one pontiff in Avignon, recognized by France, Spain, and the Kingdom of Sicily, and another pope in Rome, recognized by most of Italy and the other monarchs. This situation was not resolved until the Council of Constance, convened in 1413, after which there was only one pontiff, Martin V.

For how long was the Papal Palace of Avignon the seat of the Catholic Church?

For 67 years. Six conclaves were held there.

After the Avignon period, where did the popes live?

When the pope returned to Rome in 1377, he found the Lateran Palace in such a bad state that he preferred to move first to the basilica of Santa Maria in Trastevere, in the Roman neighborhood of that name, subsequently to the basilica of Santa Maria Maggiore and finally to the Vatican.

What were the Papal States?

The Papal States were territories that belonged to the Church through supposed donations and acquisitions to guarantee the sovereignty and autonomy of the Pope. Although they received several names, their beginning can be fixed in the year 756, and their end in 1870. It had as names "Patrimony of St. Peter", "Pontifical State", "Ecclesiastical State" and "State of the Church".

As a political unit, it was born after the fall of the Byzantine Empire, when the Pope and the bishops began to consolidate their role as key figures for the provision of goods and the administration of justice, and progressively acquired the rest of the civil powers. Geographically it occupied practically a third of the Italian peninsula. In the 16th century it extended for 44,000 kilometers. On the eve of its disappearance, in 1870, it reached 12,000 square kilometers.

Like any country, it had to face attacks from other states and was defeated four times. After the Vatican troops assassinated a general of the French embassy, in 1798 the French army invaded the Papal States, proclaimed the first Roman Republic and captured Pope Pius VI, who died a prisoner in France.

What effects did the proclamation in 1798 of the first Roman Republic have on the Catholic Church?

Politically, for a year and almost seven months (from February 15, 1798, to September 30, 1799) the Papal States were dissolved and the temporal power of the popes was eliminated. Pope Pius VI was arrested by order of Napoleon and sent to France, where he died on August 29, 1799, and the cardinals were expelled from Rome

The Roman Republic was a satellite state of Paris that sought to export Jacobin ideas. The new authorities of this territory closed the monasteries and recognized civil marriage and divorce. The situation changed when on September 19, 1799, the French troops left Rome because of the siege they were suffering in all the frontiers of the Republic. Eleven days later the Neapolitan troops entered, liberated the Eternal City and the republican laws were abrogated. Two years later, in 1801, Napoleon's France and the Holy See signed a concordat.

But Napoleon tried again to get rid of the pope and in July 1809 he again took possession of the Papal States and arrested Pius VII. The pontiff would recover the Papal States thanks to Napoleon's military defeats, when during the Congress of Vienna, in 1815, the new borders of Europe were agreed upon and his jurisdiction over the Papal States was recognized. The Pope also ceded a strip of his territory to Austria.

Was there a second Roman Republic?

Yes, the Papal States were closed again a few years later. Despite Napoleon's military defeat, liberal revolutions had spread throughout Europe, and the population of the Papal States insistently asked the pontiff for political reforms that would take these new ideas on board. It meant, for example, the withdrawal of privileges from the upper classes and a more democratic government. The timid measures launched by the pope did not convince the population.

The situation precipitated in Rome, where protests degenerated into violence. Pope Pius IX had to escape by night on November 24, 1848, dressed as a priest, and took refuge in Gaeta, south of Rome. From there, he requested the protection of the Kingdom of the Two Sicilies and called on the Catholic powers (France, Austria, Spain and the Kingdom of the Two Sicilies) to come to his aid.

On February 9, an assembly of representatives of the people decreed in Rome that "the papacy has lost de facto and de jure the temporal government of the Roman State" and announced the birth of the Roman Republic. It did state that "the Roman Pontiff shall have all the necessary guarantees of independence in the exercise of his spiritual power". Universal suffrage was granted to men, the death penalty was abolished, and freedom of worship was established.

The Roman Republic lasted five months. It was dissolved on July 4, 1849, when French troops, sent to protect the pope, intervened. Pius IX returned to Rome on April 12, 1850.

Is it true that a pope was invited to take up residence in Mexico?

When in 1848 Pope Pius IX had to leave Rome and seek refuge in Gaeta, the Mexican Congress sent him a letter inviting him to take up residence in Chapultepec Castle. The message was signed by President José Joaquín Herrera, who had been elected on February 2 of the same year[1].

1. Francisco Ramírez Meza and Fr. Manuel Olimón.

When did the Popes definitively lose temporal power and the Papal States disappear?

After 1815, the spirit of the French Revolution and the ideas of "liberty, equality and fraternity" spread throughout Europe and were consolidated also in the Papal States. In the territory of the Italian peninsula, these ideas were joined by the project of building a new country that would unite the entire peninsula

Thus, the Piedmontese gradually annexed territories of the Papal States by means of plebiscites in the cities, which rose up one by one against the authority of the pope. Thus, in 1860, the Papal States included only the city of Rome and its surroundings, where French troops remained to protect Pope Pius IX.

The situation changed again when the Prussian wars forced the French army to retreat, and the pope was left unprotected. On September 20, 1870, the Piedmontese army invaded Rome. The artillery broke through the resistance at the Porta Pia and entered the city. The Swiss guard and the papal soldiers or "bersaglieri" tried to resist, but the pope gave orders that no blood should be shed. That same day, the Papal State surrendered, and the white flag was raised in St. Peter's Square. In practice it was the last gesture of that country.

From then on, Rome became the capital of united Italy, and the Savoy royal family moved to the papal palace of the Quirinal.

How did the Pope react to the loss of the Papal States?

Very badly. Pius IX continued to consider himself the usurped sovereign of the Papal State. Therefore, he locked himself in the Vatican, from where he never left, and declared himself a prisoner of the Italian State, which he considered an illegitimate invader. He refused any agreement with the new government.

In time it was seen that the loss of temporal power spared Peter's successors the delicate task of governing and protecting territory, maintaining an army, declaring and facing wars, imposing taxes and issuing civil laws. From then on, their spiritual character and moral strength was reinforced.

How long was the pope a "prisoner" in the Vatican?

The situation lasted from 1870 to 1929, that is, almost 60 years. Pius IX declared himself a "prisoner of the Italian State," and his successors (Leo XIII, Pius X and Benedict XV) maintained the rule of not leaving the Vatican confines as a gesture of rejection of the Piedmontese invasion. They also asked Italian Catholics not to intervene in the political life of the unified country. The new Italian government had offered generous solutions, such as the "Law of Guarantees", but the pontiffs did not accept any possibility that would leave them without a relevant sovereign territory. Thus, when they were elected pope, they did not go to St. Peter's Square to greet the pilgrims, but to an interior balcony that does not face Rome.

In 1922, Pius XI wanted to reduce the tension and, as soon as he was elected, he broke with the tradition of his predecessors and leaned out on the external balcony of St. Peter's. Later, during the Fascist government of Mussolini, he agreed to seek an agreement with the Italian government. Representatives for the negotiations were appointed on August 26, 1926.

As a result, the Lateran Treaty, signed on February 11, 1929, recognized the pope's full sovereignty over a tiny territory around St. Peter's Basilica, the Vatican City State, and a series of economic compensations for the expropriated resources (mines, agricultural land, buildings), to guarantee its present and future independence. This put an end to the controversy. The pacts were revised in 1984, to eliminate, among other things, the mention of Catholicism as a state religion in Italy.

Who signed the Lateran Treaty?

It was signed by the then Secretary of State of the Holy See, Cardinal Pietro Gasparri, on behalf of Pius XI, and Italian Prime Minister Benito Mussolini, on behalf of King Victor Emmanuel III.

The Holy See

What is the difference between the Vatican and the Holy See?

They are different entities, and it is a mistake to confuse them. On the one hand, the Vatican is the civil, geopolitical State, endowed with borders, whose monarch is the Pope; on the other hand, the Holy See is the government that the successor of St. Peter exercises over the entire Catholic Church.

The Latin word "*sedes*" means chair or throne and refers to the place from which one governs or teaches. Thus, the "Holy See" is the area governed by the pontiff.

What types of laws does the pope promulgate, as an exercise of government?

The pope governs the Vatican City State and the Holy See with different types of laws depending on the area covered. Depending on the importance of the question addressed, its development and scope, and its addressees, the pope may choose to issue a Motu Proprio, a Bull or Brief, an Apostolic Letter, an Apostolic Exhortation, an Apostolic Constitution, an Encyclical Epistle, or an Encyclical Letter.

What is a Motu Proprio?

It is a document with provisions or norms that the pope issues on his own initiative and not in response to a request, nor at the request of others. In general, the legal determinations that appear in this type of document have the full force of papal authority, although they do not abrogate existing laws, unless specified.

What is a Papal Bull?

It is a papal decree for specific and delimited matters, such as appointing a new bishop, granting a dispensation, announcing an excommunication, certifying a canonization, or convoking an important event.

Its name derives from the wax or metal seal ("*bulla*") that the Pope's chancellery has used since the 6th century to authenticate these documents. This metal seal could be lead, but also gold. In the Middle Ages, it was used by monarchs and princes to authenticate their edicts and agreements between nobles. Gradually, its use was limited to papal decisions of doctrinal or disciplinary importance.

Until the 11th century the material of the bulls was parchment or papyrus. From then on, only parchment or "vellum", which is the skin of stillborn or newborn calves, was used[2].

On the front of the seal was a cross and a representation of St. Peter and St. Paul, while on the back

2. Vellum is a type of parchment that was used to make the pages of a book or codex, characterized by its thinness, durability and smoothness. Strictly speaking, vellum paper should only be made of calfskin (vellum), but the term began to be used to designate a very high quality parchment. Most manuscripts of the Middle Ages, both illustrated and unillustrated, were written on vellum paper.

was the name of the pope who signed it and the year of the current pontificate. This seal or "bull" was attached to the document by means of a hemp rope or a red or yellow silk ribbon.

What is an Apostolic Brief?

The "Briefs" were used as papal governing documents starting from the pontificate of Eugene IV, in the 15th century. It is a legal document less extensive than the bull, with which the pontiff addresses very specific issues or communicates resolutions quickly and without formality. It usually has no preamble or preface and mentions only one issue; for example, a "Brief" announced the closing of the Second Vatican Council on December 8, 1965. The document is signed by the pope and endorsed with the imprint of the Fisherman's ring.

What is an Apostolic Constitution?

It is the highest legal norm issued by the Supreme Pontiff and is used for definitive teachings or provisions of major importance. The word "constitution" evokes civil law, while the appellative "apostolic" underlines that it is promulgated by the "Apostolic See".

John Paul II used this modality to establish the rules of the Sede Vacante and the Conclave. Francis issued in March 2022 an "Apostolic Constitution" on the organization of the Vatican Curia. There are also apostolic constitutions of less importance to institute new dioceses.

Ecumenical Councils, the assembly that brings together all the bishops of the world, also have the power to issue an "Apostolic Constitution". The Second Vatican Council published both dogmatic (the texts "Lumen Gentium", on the Church, and "Dei Verbum", on the Bible) and pastoral (the texts "Gaudium et Spes", on the contemporary world, and "Sacrosanctum Concilium", on the liturgy) "Apostolic Constitutions".

What is an Apostolic Letter?

It is a document of magisterial character of lesser solemnity. It usually consists of a reflection on general questions, often with a spiritual focus. John Paul II wrote one in 1988 on the dignity of women ("Mulieris Dignitatem"), and one in 2003 on the Eucharist ("Mane Nobiscum Domine"). Benedict XVI wrote an apostolic letter in 2011 to convoke the "Year of Faith". Francis has written them on the Christmas crib ("Admirabile signum", 2019), on St. Joseph ("Patris corde", 2020), and on Blaise Pascal ("Sublimitas et miseria hominis", 2023).

It can also be used for the promulgation of a papal act, such as declaring a new "doctor of the Church", or elevating a temple to the category of basilica.

What is an Apostolic Exhortation?

It is a category of magisterial document similar to an encyclical, which the pope uses to communicate specific contents or conclusions to the Catholic Church or to a specific group of Catholics after having considered the recommendations of a synod. In terms of subject matter, the most recent encyclicals have dealt with holiness in daily life, the conclusions of a synod of bishops and the pastoral care of families.

One of Francis' first documents was the Apostolic Exhortation "Evangelii Gaudium" (2013), in which he set out the program of his pontificate. John Paul II wrote one in 1996 with advice and indications for the consecrated life. Benedict XVI wrote four, with the conclusions of various synods.

What is an Encyclical?

The term has the same root as the word "encyclopedia". It comes from the Latin "encyclia" and the Greek ἐκκύκλιος ("egkyklios") meaning "circular" or "general". It is a "circular letter."

In the ancient Christian Church it was a letter sent by any bishop to the faithful of a specific area. The Orthodox and Anglican Churches still use the term with that meaning, but since Benedict XIV (1740-1758), the Catholic Church uses it only for papal texts. It is a letter from the pontiff to Catholics, and in general extends "to all people of good will".

The content, generally doctrinal, social or pastoral, can be very varied. For example, the implications of work in Catholic social doctrine, the protection of life, the relationship between Science and Faith, the theological virtues or the coexistence of different cultures.

The pontiff defines when and under what circumstances it should be sent. The popes have recourse to them with different intensity. Benedict XIV published 4; Pius VII, 1; Pius IX, 1; Leo XIII, 3; St. Pius X, 2; Benedict XV, 2; Pius XI, 8; Pius XII made 41. John XXIII published 8; Paul VI, 7; John Paul II, 14; and Benedict XVI, 3. Francis has published 4 encyclicals.

The official text is usually in Latin and is titled with the same words with which it begins.

When addressing Catholics specifically, the Pope usually writes an "Apostolic Exhortation" instead of an encyclical.

How is the Holy See organized?

To carry out his religious, political and humanitarian work, the pope is assisted by various departments, called the "Vatican Curia" or "Roman Curia". These are "Tribunals" and "Dicasteries", equivalent in the religious sphere to ministries of the government of a nation.

What is the organizational structure of the Holy See?

The number one in the organizational structure of the Holy See would be the pope. He is followed by the heads of the most important departments of the Vatican Curia. Thus, number two is the Secretary of State, and number three, the Substitute of the Secretariat of State, who concretizes and coordinates the work of the dicasteries.

What organizations make up the Vatican Curia?

The Vatican Curia is coordinated by the Secretariat of State, and is composed of Tribunals, Dicasteries and other bodies. These are specifically:

1) The Secretariat of State, which is responsible for the internal coordination of the Curia, for the political implementation of the Pope's decisions, and for the Holy See's diplomatic relations with other states and with nunciatures.

2) The Dicasteries, which are sixteen large departments that assist the Pope in specific matters. They are these:

- Dicastery for Evangelization
- Dicastery for the Doctrine of the Faith
- Dicastery for the Service of Charity
- Dicastery for the Eastern Churches
- Dicastery for Divine Worship and the Discipline of the Sacraments
- Dicastery for the Causes of Saints
- Dicastery for Bishops
- Dicastery for the Clergy
- Dicastery for Institutes of Consecrated Life and Societies of Apostolic Life
- Dicastery for the Laity, the Family and Life
- Dicastery for the Promotion of Christian Unity
- Dicastery for Interreligious Dialogue
- Dicastery for Culture and Education

- Dicastery for the Service of Integral Human Development
- Dicastery for Legislative Texts
- Dicastery for Communication.

3) The Holy See also has three tribunals: the Apostolic Penitentiary, the Apostolic Signatura and the Roman Rota.

4) In addition, it has a number of specialized bodies for financial management: Council for the Economy, Secretariat for the Economy, Administration of the Patrimony of the Apostolic See, Office of the Auditor General, Commission for Reserved Matters, the Investment Committee and the Authority for Supervision and Financial Information.

5) There are three small departments that deal with non-executive matters: the Prefecture of the Papal Household, the Office of the Liturgical Celebrations of the Supreme Pontiff, the Camerlengo of the Holy Roman Church.

In addition to all of these, there are other non-governmental organizations of great importance. These are the Vatican Apostolic Archives, the Vatican Apostolic Library, the Fabric of St. Peter, the Pontifical Commission for Sacred Archaeology and the Pontifical Academies of Sciences, Social Sciences and Life.

What are "Dicasteries"?

The name derives from the term "dicasterion", the people's court of Athens in ancient Greece, which served to control the decrees voted by the Athenian assembly.

The dicasteries in the ecclesiastical sphere are the large departments of the Vatican Curia that carry out their work in the name of the Pope and under his authority. There are currently sixteen dicasteries.

Each is concerned with the governance and oversight of a specific sector of the Catholic Church's activity, such as the process of appointing bishops, the judgment of candidates for sainthood, liturgical matters, the spiritual life of the laity, or religious congregations.

What is referred to as the Peter's Pence?

This name is given to the financial support that the Church, concretely through dioceses around the world but also through donations from the faithful, offers annually to the Pope to cover the expenses for the governing of the Holy See and to contribute to the alms that he gives. It is usually collected on June 29, feast of the Apostles Peter and Paul.

Does the Church need the pope to survive?

Theologically, the survival of the Church does not depend on the pope but on God and is guaranteed by Him. In fact, the Church has remained for long periods without a pontiff and in that time, bishops, priests and laity have continued to pray, preach, live the Gospel message, celebrate the Holy Mass and the other sacraments, as well as organize in various areas and do works of charity.

During the time when popes have been exiled or imprisoned to prevent them from exercising their functions, or the See has been vacant, the Holy Spirit has not ceased to breathe on the work founded by Christ.

That said, Catholics consider that Jesus' mission to Peter, "You are Peter, and on this 'rock' I will build my Church," "Feed my lambs," leaves no doubt as to Christ's will that there should be a pontiff. The necessary presence of the pope as visible head, as successor of Peter, as elder brother in the faith, as the one who convokes and encourages as a good shepherd, provides the indispensable unity in the Church.

The Vatican City State

Does private property exist in the Vatican?

No, there is no private property. The Vatican City State is an absolute elective monarchy that does not levy taxes, does not allow private ownership of land and does not recognize the right to vote. This country exists specifically to ensure the freedom of the Pope to carry out his mission in the service of the Church. Within its borders, everything belongs to the Holy See and everything (land, houses, instruments, etc.), is intended to help the pope fulfill his task without external pressure. That is why there is no private property.

What taxes do Vatican citizens pay?

The Vatican City State does not collect taxes. It provides its employees with jobs, health care and pensions. It also deducts some pension and health premiums. They do not pay taxes such as VAT or other fiscal charges, because it is not part of the European Community.

Does the Vatican have stores?

Within the Vatican City State there are a few stores, such as those at the Vatican Museums, a grocery store, a wholesale merchandise store, and the cheapest gas station in Rome, which can only be used by Vatican employees and which discounts taxes added by the Italian State.

Does the Vatican City State issue birth certificates?

Because of its peculiar legislation, although the Vatican is a State, it does not issue birth certificates. If a child were born in the Vatican City State, he would have documentation from Italy.

Do priests have a Vatican passport?

No. Every priest is a citizen of the place where he was born or of the country where he resides. Those who live in the Vatican do not lose their nationality and in some cases may have, depending on their work or position, a temporary passport of the Vatican City State.

Who designed the Vatican flag?

The current flag was designed by Pope Pius VII in 1808. Until then it used the colors amaranth (yellow) and red, representing the Senate and the Roman People. The city of Rome still uses these colors. The flag is square and has the colors white and yellow. In the white part it has the triple crown and the crossed keys, symbol of the Holy See.

What does the coat of arms of the Holy See symbolize?

The coat of arms of the Holy See shows two keys, one golden and the other silver. The keys recall the words Christ said to Peter: "I will give you the keys to the kingdom of heaven. Whatever you bind on earth shall be bound in heaven; and whatever you loose on earth shall be loosed in heaven"[3].

The golden key evokes the power in Heaven, and the silver key the power on earth, but it does not refer to the common interpretation of "power", as if it were "dominion", but to its Christian sense, which considers it a "service". The colors gold and silver can be reduced to yellow and white.

Sometimes the coat of arms is enriched with the papal tiara, a triple crown used by the pontiffs until Paul VI.

In addition to this general coat of arms, like every bishop or archbishop, the pope may have his own coat of arms, which will accompany him during his pontificate. Benedict replaced the crown or tiara in his coat of arms with a miter, to emphasize that he was a bishop and not a monarch. Francis continued this custom.

What is the Swiss Guard?

The Swiss Guard was founded by Pope Julius II, Giuliano della Rovere, on January 21, 1506, with

3. Mt 16, 19

the mission to protect the successor of Peter. It was formed by 150 Swiss mercenaries thanks to the great reputation they had earned in the Burgundian Wars. Since then, it has been the military corps at the service of the pontiffs.

It fulfilled one of its most heroic gestures on May 6, 1527, when they defended the pope from the attack of a thousand German and Spanish soldiers. It was during the Sack of Rome by the troops of Emperor Charles V, carried out in retaliation for a maneuver of the pontiff and the king of France to seize territories in Italy from the Habsburg emperor. The Swiss guards fought in front of St. Peter's Basilica and continued fighting inside, while retreating to the steps of the high altar, where Pope Clement VII was praying. In the midst of the fighting, they convinced him to escape through an 800-meter passageway leading to the castle of Sant'Angelo. Pope Clement was saved, but only 42 of the 189 Swiss guards survived: in the passageway in the middle of the attack, dozens of guards protecting him lost their lives, including one who had disguised himself as a pontiff to confuse the attackers.

In remembrance of this fact, every May 6, new recruits of the Swiss Guard are sworn in by a representative of the pope and those who have received a promotion step into their new position.

What is the role of the Swiss Guard?

It is the army of the sovereign State of Vatican City. It is in charge of protecting the Pope and guarding his residence, the Apostolic Palace and Casa Santa Marta. They also form the picket of honor when there is a State visit to the Vatican, and in case of "Sede Vacante", they are in charge of guaranteeing the security of the college of cardinals.

How many troops does the Swiss Guard have?

This military corps is composed of some 135 troops: the Commander of the Swiss Guard, with the rank of colonel, the Vice Commander of the Swiss Guard and a chaplain, an officer with the rank of Commander, two officers with the rank of Captain, 23 middle commanders, 70 halberdiers and two drummers.

How is the Swiss Guard trained?

Although the Vatican is a pacifist state, its guards are trained to handle modern weapons such as the Swiss SIG 550 rifle and SIG P225 pistols. They receive lessons in self-defense and instruction in defensive bodyguard tactics for the protection of heads of state. Some claim that each Swiss guard hides a tear gas sprayer in his uniform and, from the rank of sergeant upwards, a pistol and two grenades.

Who designed the Swiss Guard uniform?

Many think that Michelangelo designed his uniform, when the merit belongs to Major Jules Répond, who modernized the Swiss Guard in the early twentieth century and was inspired by some frescoes by Raphael in the Apostolic Palace to design the dresses and helmets of his soldiers.

The blue and yellow colors are those of the coat of

arms of Julius II, the pope who instituted this military corps. The red is that of the Medici, in memory of Clement VII, whom they heroically protected in 1527. The flag of the guard has on the lower part the arms of Julius II and, on the upper part, those of the pope who at that time governs the Church.

What are the requirements to join the Swiss Guard?

The requirements to be part of the Swiss Guard are to be male, single, have Swiss citizenship, be Catholic and have passed military service. In addition, they must be taller than 1.74 m, between 19 and 30 years of age, have a high school diploma and a driver's license. They must pass a physical and psychological health test that evaluates their ability to withstand stress, and have no criminal record or financial problems. Once admitted, recruits commit themselves to two months of training and to serve in the Vatican for at least 24 months. Until a few years ago, only officers were allowed to marry. Those over 25 years of age, who have been in the army for at least five years and who are committed to serve for another three years, are now allowed to marry.

Vatican Sites

What is a basilica?

In the times of the Roman Empire, "basilica" was the name given to large public buildings destined to administer justice, to do business or for social activities. They were perhaps the busiest places in the forum, had a rectangular plan with a facade of arches and an open interior, with rows of large columns supporting the roof and dividing several naves. To get an idea of their structure, the remains of the "Basilica Julia", dating from the first century B.C., or the "Basilica Emilia", dating from the second century B.C., are preserved in the Roman Forum.

In 313, the Edict of Milan made Christian worship possible in the Roman Empire, and Christians went from worshipping in private homes to worshipping in public buildings. At that time, they were inspired by the Roman basilicas to build their temples, and these Christian basilicas became the successors of the small "domus ecclesiae" or domestic churches. Thus, they acquired a function different from the one they had had previously, as they became places of worship.

How did the great Christian basilicas of Rome come into being?

When on October 28, 312, Emperor Constantine won the battle of Milvian Bridge against Maxentius, he wanted to pay homage to the divinity that had brought about the victory, which he attributed to the God of the Christians, and had a temple built over the tomb of the apostle Peter, a place of reference for the Christian community of Rome.

Later, three other Christian basilicas were erected in Rome: St. John Lateran, which served as the Pope's cathedral, St. Paul Outside the Walls, over the tomb of the apostle Paul, and St. Mary Major, which was the first great temple dedicated to the Virgin Mary in the city. These four basilicas remain today the most important for Christians in the Eternal City, and those who visit them receive special graces and indulgences. They alone receive the title of "Major Basilicas."

There are some other churches throughout the world that, by decision of the pope, are linked to the Basilica of St. John Lateran, almost as if they were its branches. In them one can receive the same graces and privileges as in the cathedral of Rome. These buildings are given the title of "minor basilicas".

Who built the first St. Peter's Basilica?

Emperor Constantine consulted the Christians where they wanted to build a temple in Rome, because he wanted to thank their God for his help in obtaining victory in the battle of Milvian Bridge. The then pope, Sylvester I, proposed that it should be erected on the Vatican Hill, over tomb of the apostle Peter which was in an ancient necropolis. According to tradition, work began between 319 and 326 and was completed around 333.

Is the current St. Peter's Basilica the same one built by Emperor Constantine?

No, but they are in the same place. Constantine approved the idea of building a Christian basilica on the tomb of St. Peter. This first basilica was imposing. It had five naves and was decorated with mosaics and columns evoking those of the temple of Jerusalem. It had a mosaic in the apse with Christ flanked by St. Peter and St. Paul. Over the centuries it continued to be completed. For example, at the end of the 4th century a portico with four entrances was added to the façade.

After almost a thousand years of existence, at the end of the 14th century, the building was in such a bad state that the pontiffs Martin V and Eugene IV considered reforms. At the beginning of the 16th century, Julius II opted to demolish it definitively and rebuild it from scratch. He himself laid the first stone on April 17, 1506. His successors Paul III, Sixtus V and Paul V put special interest in accelerating its construction and contributed very significant elements. Paul III called Michelangelo to make the dome; under Sixtus V it was completed, and the Vatican obelisk was erected; and Paul V inaugurated the façade and put his name on it.

St. Peter's Basilica is probably the largest Catholic church in the world at 211.50 meters long and 132.50 meters high. Its dome has a diameter of 42 meters.

Is it true that part of the Colosseum was demolished to build the new St. Peter's Basilica?

No, this is not true. At the end of the 15th century, after the papal period in Avignon, the first basilica of St. Peter was very deteriorated and threatened to collapse. In 1452, Pope Nicholas V considered rebuilding it or at least making radical changes so that it would not collapse on its own, and commissioned Leon Battista Alberti and Bernardo Rossellino to carry out the work. That pope approved that the materials of the Colosseum that had already collapsed during the earthquake of 1349 be systematically extracted to be used in new constructions. In a single year, they transported 2,500 carts of travertine.

The material fallen from the Colosseum continued to be used for buildings in Rome long after the completion of the work on the basilica. For example, in 1634 for the Palazzo Barberini and, after a new earthquake, in 1703, for the port of Ripetta, on the banks of the Tiber.

Where is the tomb of St. Peter?

The tomb of St. Peter is several meters below the main altar of St. Peter's Basilica. The Vatican dome, 136 meters high, was built to mark the exact spot where it is located.

How was Peter's tomb located in St. Peter's Basilica?

We know that St. Peter was buried in the year 64 or 67 in a necropolis located outside the Circus of Nero, on the Vatican Hill, next to the Via Cornelia, which is less than 150 meters from the place of his martyrdom.

With the passage of time, that tomb was highlighted with a small red stone wall, which evoked his name "*petrus*" and served for Christians to identify it. A small roof was built over it, like a hermitage. The "old basilica of St. Peter" or Constantinian basilica was built on top of that exact place in the middle of the 4th century. About eleven centuries later, in 1506, in view of the danger of collapse, Pope Julius II authorized the demolition of that ancient basilica and the construction of the present one, crowned with Michelangelo's dome. Out of respect for St. Peter, his tomb was not tampered with during either of the two constructions.

In 1939 Pius XI died and in his will he asked to be buried as close as possible to the tomb of the first pope, Peter. This allowed his successor, Pius XII, to authorize an archaeological investigation to locate the remains of the tomb of the apostle. Until then, no pope had ever ordered such a thing.

For ten years they excavated to unearth the ancient necropolis, a burial area that existed before the construction of Nero's circus and which is under the present basilica. In addition to Roman citizens, the victims of the circus executions were buried there, and later many Christians who wished to be buried near St. Peter.

Excavations revealed the remains of the three altars that were built successively in the times of Gregory I (590-604), Callixtus II (1123) and Clement VIII (1594) over a small tomb. The superimposition of altars confirmed that since the 6th century pilgrims have identified this place as the tomb of the apostle Peter.

Once informed of the archaeologists' findings, on December 23, 1950, Pope Pius XII announced the discovery of the tomb of St. Peter. Fragments of bones and the remains of a purple and gold cloth in which they had probably been wrapped had also been preserved there. Although it is impossible to determine with absolute certainty that they were the remains of Peter, the cloth did correspond to a personage of great importance.

Is it possible to visit the tomb of St. Peter?

Yes, although the tomb is located several levels below the present basilica, it is possible to visit it with a special permit. Scholars or visitors descend into the area of the ancient necropolis accompanied by a specialist who explains the area. The visit lasts approximately one hour. Other pilgrims can see from St. Peter's Basilica the red wall indicating the area of the tomb of the apostle. They can also celebrate mass on a small altar above Peter's tomb and under the papal altar.

What are the so-called Patriarchal or Papal Basilicas?

These are the four ancient basilicas linked to the history of the first Christian communities in the eternal city. They are St. John Lateran (Cathedral of Rome), St. Peter's in the Vatican, St. Paul Outside the Walls, on Via Ostiense, and St. Mary Major, on the Esquiline Hill. All are characterized by a Holy Door and a papal altar. John Paul II asked that they be called "Papal Basilicas".

What is the Apostolic Palace?

It is the "Papal Palace" of the Vatican. It is the official residence of the pontiffs and the place where they receive official visits. It began to be built at the end of the 15th century, after the return of the popes from Avignon. In addition to the "Papal Apartment", where John Paul II died and where Benedict XVI resided, the complex of buildings includes the offices of the central government of the Catholic Church, chapels for the celebration of ceremonies and the conclave, the Vatican Museums and the Vatican Library and Archives. In total, there are approximately 1,000 rooms.

Every Sunday at 12 noon, the Pope looks out of a window of the Apostolic Palace overlooking the square, which is from the study of the Pontiff's private apartment, to pray the Angelus with pilgrims.

In 2013 Pope Francis chose to move his residence, in a personal capacity, to Casa Santa Marta, a place where other priests who work at the Vatican and people who visit the Holy See for work purposes also stay. Francis used the Vatican Apostolic Palace as the seat of representation of the Pontiff, and there he held audiences and meetings with heads of state, heads of government and ambassadors.

Which papal residences are there in Rome?

There are two other papal residences in and around Rome, the Palazzo Lateranense or the Lateran and the Villa Barberini in Castel Gandolfo.

Until 1870, when the Papal States fell, the Pope's summer residence was the Quirinal Palace in Rome. This place was confiscated in 1871 by the King of Italy who made it his official residence. Since 1946, with the abolition of the Italian monarchy, this palace has been the residence of the President of the Italian Republic.

What is the Lateran Palace?

For about a thousand years, the Lateran Palace was the official residence of the pope in Rome. It is next to the Basilica of St. John Lateran, which is the cathedral of Rome. Its construction dates back to the times of the Roman Empire, since according to tradition, this area was given in the early fourth century to Pope Sylvester by the Emperor Constantine himself. The place corresponded to the barracks of his rival, Maxentius, defeated in 312 in the battle of Milvian Bridge. Six councils were held there between 1123 and 1517.

Around the 10th century it was badly damaged by a terrible fire and then rebuilt; it was later embellished by Pope Innocent III. When the papal see had to move to Avignon, France, the palace entered a period of decay augmented by further fires in 1307 and 1361; and when the pontiffs returned to Rome, they no longer resided in it.

It currently houses the Pontifical Museum of Christian Antiquities. It still has papal apartments although they are no longer in use.

What is referred to as St. Peter's Square?

When the current St. Peter's Basilica was completed, in front of its façade there was a large outer space without order or shape. Pope Alexander VII had the idea of shaping it to serve as an antechamber to the temple and to welcome pilgrims. Thus, in 1656 he asked Bernini to design this square.

First, Bernini designed a rectangular space surrounded by porticoes, with the idea that the Vatican would build palaces over them and rent them out to cover the hole left in its coffers by the work on the new basilica and Michelangelo's dome. The pontiff responded that real estate speculation in the heart of Catholicism was inappropriate, and asked him to find a different approach

The artist then conceived of a square in the shape of an ellipse, delimited by a colonnade that evokes the way in which the Church welcomes all people, regardless of their religion. In the archives of the "Fabbrica di San Pietro", the body that cares for this site, is preserved the draft that Bernini prepared to explain his design. He wrote: "*...A portico showing that it receives with maternally open arms Catholics, to confirm them in their faith; heretics, to bring them back to the Church; and infidels, to enlighten them in the true faith*".

The square is built very close to one end of the ancient Circus of Nero, now disappeared. It is certain that St. Peter was assassinated there. The only witness that remains of that tragedy was the obelisk that stands in the center of the present square, which was in the Roman circus, and that the first apostle could see when he was led there for his crucifixion.

The square is delimited by 284 white marble columns, each 16 meters high. At the top of the colonnade there are 140 statues of saints, "columns" of the Church. To give symmetry to the whole, at each end of the square there is a fountain.

This place has been the scene of emblematic moments in the history of the Catholic Church, such as the closing of the Second Vatican Council in 1965 or the assassination attempt on John Paul II in 1981. Here the pope celebrates certain solemn liturgies and public audiences. The most crowded ceremony in memory is the funeral of John Paul II, on April 8, 2005, when some 500,000 faithful also gathered in the surrounding streets.

What special security measures are in place in St. Peter's Square?

The square is a geopolitically unique and delicate place. Although there is no customs, its borders delimit the frontier between Italy and the Vatican City State. It occupies about 47,600 square meters. Every day it receives at least 25,000 tourists and pilgrims, a figure that is multiplied by at least four when it hosts a ceremony of the Pope.

Before the attack on John Paul II, on May 13, 1981, there were no security checkpoints during the audiences. Since then, controls were activated to access meetings with the Bishop of Rome. Since 2000, pilgrims and tourists must pass through the scanner, which was reinforced in 2015 after attacks in Paris.

Why is there an obelisk in St. Peter's Square?

It is an Egyptian obelisk of the nineteenth century BC, almost 26 meters high and weighing 327 tons. It was in the city of Heliopolis and was moved to Rome in the year 40 by order of the emperor Caligula and arranged to mark the center of the Circus of Nero, precisely where St. Peter was martyred.

This Roman circus was destroyed centuries later, also with the construction of St. Peter's Basilica by Emperor Constantine, but the heavy obelisk was preserved in place. It is the only obelisk in Rome that has always remained standing.

In 1586 Pope Sixtus V decided to place it in front of the basilica in memory of the martyrdom of the apostle Peter and other Christians of the first centuries. It is known as the "mute witness", as it witnessed these executions and is one of the last points that Peter looked at before dying.

At its apex was a bronze sphere which, according to medieval legend, contained the remains of Julius Caesar. It is preserved in the Capitoline Museums. It was replaced by a crucifix, to which a relic of the cross of Christ was added in 1740.

What is the Via della Conciliazione?

The Avenue of Reconciliation, or in Italian "Via della Conciliazione" is an avenue in the Borgo district of Rome. It connects St. Peter's Square with the western bank of the Tiber River and with the Castle of Sant'Angelo (Castel Sant'Angelo). It was built between 1936 and 1950, to commemorate the signing of the Lateran Agreements between Italy and the Holy See that put an end to the controversy between the two after the fall of the Papal States.

To build it, dozens of buildings had to be demolished, because it occupies the area that until then housed the "borgo", an ancient medieval quarter. These houses concealed the basilica, which appeared by surprise after crossing the colonnade. For the pilgrims, it was a magnificent experience, as they emerged from narrow streets and passed through ancient buildings and found themselves almost by surprise in front of the imposing building.

The idea of building an avenue linking the basilica to the Tiber came from Benito Mussolini, who announced the decision on April 21, 1934, the anniversary of the founding of Rome, a holiday of the Fascist regime that exploited the ideals of ancient "*Romanitas*". Later, he himself supervised the works.

Today it is very functional because it is a useful valve to accommodate thousands of pilgrims and visitors who come daily to the Vatican. It is about 420 meters long and is the main and fastest access route to St. Peter's Square. On its sides it hosts stores, embassies and buildings of historical and religious value. The best known are the Palazzo Torlonia - the only one in the area that retains its original location -, the Palazzo dei Penitenzieri, the Palazzo dei Convertendi and the church of Santa Maria in Traspontina.

Where does the pope celebrate daily mass?

The pope usually celebrates Mass every day in his own chapel, early in the morning. Depending on the circumstances, he may do so privately, with a small group of companions, or by himself.

When there is an important solemnity or feast, it is usually celebrated in St. Peter's Basilica, in the Vatican, or in some special place in Rome such as one of the other major basilicas: the Basilica of St. John Lateran, which is his cathedral; the Basilica of St. Paul Outside the Walls or the Basilica of St. Mary Major.

In addition, throughout the liturgical year he often visits other minor basilicas and parishes in Rome. And during his pastoral trips he celebrates the Eucharist in cathedrals, parishes or open spaces.

What is the Pope's cathedral?

As bishop of Rome, the pope's cathedral is the basilica (also called "archbasilica") of St. John Lateran.

On which days does the pope publicly pray the Angelus prayer?

He prays it in public every Sunday and in general on religious feast days, at 12 noon, from the window of his office in the Apostolic Palace, which overlooks St. Peter's Square. Thousands of pilgrims usually come to listen to him. He begins with a brief commentary on the Gospel of the day's Mass. He then prays this prayer aloud in Latin, gives a blessing and bids farewell to those present.

The first time he prayed it from his window and with pilgrims was on August 15, 1954, at the idea of the then president of Catholic Action in Italy, Luigi Gedda. On that day Pius XII prayed an Angelus that was broadcast live on Vatican Radio.

If on a Sunday the pope is outside Rome, he prays it from wherever he is, always at noon.

What is the Angelus?

The Angelus is a prayer that recalls the visit that the Archangel Gabriel made to the Virgin Mary to announce to her that she would become the mother of the Messiah, her affirmative answer and the Incarnation of the Son of God in her womb. It takes its name from the beginning of the Latin prayer: "*Angelus Domini nuntiavit Mariæ*". It is composed of three acclamations interspersed with three "Hail Marys". The Latin text prayed by the Pope is this:

1. Ángelus Dómini nuntiavit Maríae
   Et concépit de spíritu Sancto
   Ave María...

2. Ecce ancílla Dómini
   Fiat mihi secúndum verbum tuum
   Ave María...

3. Et Verbum caro factum est
   Et habitávit in nobis
   Ave María...

Ora pro nobis sancta Dei Genitrix
Ut digni efficiámur promissiónibus Christi

Orémus

Grátiam tuam, quaesumus, Dómine, méntibus nostris infúnde; ut qui, angelo nuntiánte, Christi Fílii tui incarnatiónem cognóvimus, per passiónem ejus et crucem, ad resurrectiónis glóriam perducámur. Per éumdem Christum Dóminum nostrum. Amen

The English translation is as follows:

The Angel of the Lord declared unto Mary,
And she conceived of the Holy Spirit.
Hail Mary...

Behold the handmaid of the Lord,
Be it done unto me according to your Word.
Hail Mary...

And the Word was made flesh,
And dwelt among us.
Hail Mary...

Pray for us, O Holy Mother of God, that we may be made worthy of the promises of Christ.

Let us pray.

Pour forth, we beseech you, O Lord, your grace into our hearts: that we, to whom the Incarnation of Christ your Son was made known by the message of an Angel, may by his Passion and Cross be brought to the glory of his Resurrection. Through the same Christ our Lord. Amen.

Who composed the Angelus prayer?

Some attribute the authorship of the Angelus to Pope Urban II (1042-1099) and others to Pope John XXII (1249-1334). They invited the faithful to pray it after the ringing of the bell that indicated the beginning of the day, noon or sunset. Benedict XIII (1328 - 1423) wanted to promote this prayer by granting a plenary indulgence to those who, after receiving absolution and participating in the Mass, said the Angelus at the sound of the morning, noon or evening bell. The bell ringers added some bell tolls to the Angelus to invite the faithful to pray for those who were suffering.

Others consider that the origin of the midday Angelus goes back to the prayer of three Our Fathers and three Marys which, in 1456, Pope Callixtus asked to be prayed at the sound of the bell, between three in the afternoon and sunset (approximately six o'clock), to implore the peace of the Church against the danger of the Ottoman invasion. Its popularity spread in the 16th century.

The custom of praying the Angelus three times a day is attributed to King Louis XI who in 1472 ordered its use throughout France. From there it spread to other regions of Europe.

The prayer as we know it today appears for the first time in the "Exercitum pietatis quotidianum quadripartitum", a small pious manual published in Rome under the pontificate of Pius V (1566-1572). The final triple doxology appears in the "Manuale catholicorum: in usum pie precandi" by St. Peter Canisius (1588).

During the Easter season, instead of the Angelus, the pope prays the prayer "Regina Coeli", which takes its name from the first words of the prayer in Latin.

What is the text of the Regina Caeli?

Regina caeli, laetare, alleluia.
Quia quem meruisti portare, alleluia.
Resurrexit, sicut dixit, alleluia.
Ora pro nobis Deum, alleluia.
Gaude et laetare Virgo María, alleluia.
Quia surrexit Dominus vere, alleluia.

Oremus

Deus, qui per resurrectionem Filii tui, Domini nostri Iesu Christi, mundum laetificare dignatus es: praesta, quaesumus; ut, per eius Genetricem Virginem Mariam, perpetuae capiamus gaudia vitae. Per eundem Christum Dominum nostrum. Amen.

Its English translation is:

Queen of Heaven, rejoice, alleluia.
The Son whom you merited to bear, alleluia,
has risen as he said, alleluia.
Pray for us to God; alleluia.
Rejoice and be glad, O Virgin Mary, alleluia.
For the Lord has truly risen, alleluia.

Let us pray

O God, who have been pleased to gladden the world by the Resurrection of your Son our Lord Jesus Christ, grant, we pray, that through his Mother, the Virgin Mary, we may receive the joys of everlasting life. Through Christ our Lord. Amen.

Where does the Pope hold his audiences?

The Pope receives daily private audiences with different persons or groups in the rooms of the Apostolic Palace, or in the complex of the "Paul VI Hall", or in St. Peter's Square.

Those in St. Peter's Square are the most numerous. This place is used every Wednesday early in the morning for the so-called "general audience", when weather conditions permit. In winter, or when it is a meeting with less than 8,000 people, the large audience hall, the "Paul VI Hall", is used. Before it was built, the pontiffs used the "Auditorium Conciliazione", which is now used for concerts and shows. It is at the beginning of Via della Conciliazione, was inaugurated in 1950 by Pius XII, and is the work of the architect Marcello Piacentini. In addition to audiences, in those years this place was used to screen religious films, concerts and other major events. In 1958 it became the seat of the Orchestra of the National Academy of Santa Cecilia.

In 1966, construction began within the Vatican walls on the monumental "Paul VI Hall", inaugurated on June 30, 1971, which replaced the "Auditorium Conciliazione". It is also called "Sala Nervi", in honor of the architect and engineer who designed it, Pier Luigi Nervi. The building has a trapezoidal floor plan and a curved roof with a shell-like structure, and can seat a maximum of 12,000 people, although it usually seats only about 6,500. It is conceived in such a way that visibility is good from any angle, as there are no columns inside.

On the stage there is a monumental bronze sculpture, measuring 20 by 7 by 3 meters, called "The Resurrection", a work of the artist Pericle Fazzini, created between 1970-1977. Just behind the sculpture is an organ made in 1972 by the Mascioni Company of Italy. It has five keyboards of 61 notes each, and pedals for 32 notes. The two large stained-glass windows on the sides are the work of the Hungarian-Italian artist János Hajnal. In the same complex is a small auditorium called the "New Synod Hall", with seating for about 400 people and translation booths. There are also several smaller rooms for small papal audiences, meetings and an office for the pontiff.

In 2008, thanks to a $1.5 million donation from a German company, 2,400 photovoltaic panels were installed on the roof, covering all the building's energy needs, both for air conditioning and lighting. The system won that year's European Solar Prize in the category of solar architecture and urban development. The first zero-cost papal audience was held on a cold November 26, 2008.

When the group of pilgrims does not exceed 200-300 people, the pope receives them in the "Sala Clementina" or the "Sala Ducale" of the Vatican Apostolic Palace. Other rooms of this palace dedicated to smaller meetings are the "Sala del Consistorio", where Benedict XVI communicated his resignation, or the "Sala del Tronetto", where the pope receives the credentials of the new ambassadors and greets their families.

College of Cardinals

Who are the cardinals?

They are bishops who have received special recognition from the pope, and whose main mission is to elect the new pontiff. As traditionally it was the clergy of Rome who elected him, the pope symbolically entrusts them with some parishes in the Eternal City, so that although they come from distant places or preside over Vatican dicasteries, they are "incardinated" in this city.

The Code of Canon Law devotes a chapter to explaining the functions of the cardinals[4]. It says that "they constitute a special college which provides for the election of the Roman Pontiff"[5]. Cardinals under 80 years of age are called "cardinal electors". Once they reach that age, they can no longer vote or enter the conclave, although they can participate in the previous meetings that prepare for the papal election.

They wear scarlet, a color that evokes their willingness to shed their blood to serve the pope and the Church. In addition, "they are considered Princes of the blood, with the title of Eminence"[6]. Cardinals who reside in Rome, even if outside Vatican City, have Vat-

4. Cfr. Code of Canon Law, canons. 349-359
5. Cfr. Code of Canon Law, canon. 349
6. Cfr. Historical notes on the College of Cardinals. Pontifical Yearbook 2023.

ican citizenship[7].

Apart from participating in the conclave, what other functions do the cardinals have?

Technically, their name may evoke the word "cardine", which in Italian means "hinge", because around them rotates the government of the Church. The Code of Canon Law states that one of their duties is "to cooperate assiduously with the Roman Pontiff"[8]. They are also to assist the Pope "especially in the daily care of the universal Church"[9] but only when he asks them for help. Moreover, they advise "the supreme pastor of the Church through collegial action especially in consistories in which they are gathered by mandate of the Roman Pontiff who presides"[10]. Also, each cardinal is a member of some dicasteries of the Curia to study specific questions of Church governance.

Pope Francis said that the cardinals "offer a special support to the mission of the Successor of Peter, bringing the valuable contribution of their experience and service to the particular Churches throughout the world and effectively enriching the bond of communion with the Church of Rome"[11]. For this reason, it is intended that this group include a variety of geographical and cultural backgrounds, as well as religious sensitivities.

7. Cfr. Lateran Treaty, art. 21
8. Cfr. Code of Canon Law, canon. 356
9. Code of Canon Law, canon. 349
10. Cfr. Code of Canon Law, canon. 353 § 1
11. Pope Francis' Rescript on June 26, 2018.

How has the figure of cardinals evolved throughout history?

In Rome, in the third century, the pope had seven deacons who served as a consultative and executive body for the government of the Church. Later, in the Middle Ages, the group of advisors and collaborators of the pontiff extended to "the presbyters of the 25 titular or quasi-parochial churches of Rome, the 7 (later 14) regional deacons and 6 palatine deacons and the 7 suburban bishops (in the 12th century, 6)"[12]. Little by little this body was being structured.

"From the year 1059 (the cardinals) are exclusive electors of the pope", and "from the year 1150 they formed the College of Cardinals with a Dean, who is the Bishop of Ostia, and a Camerlengo as administrator of the goods" [13]. Precisely in the twelfth century two important novelties occurred. First, the pontiffs "began also to appoint prelates residing outside Rome as cardinals"; and second, the cardinals began to hierarchically precede the bishops and archbishops, and even if they were only priests, they had the right to vote in the councils[14]. In 1439 it was established that they also preceded the patriarchs.[15].

As for the number of cardinals, in the 13th-15th centuries, there were ordinarily no more than 30. In 1586, Sixtus V established that there could be a maximum of 70 cardinals: of these, six would be cardinal bishops, fifty cardinal priests, and fourteen cardinal deacons[16]. Four centuries later, in 1958, John XXIII repealed this limit. In 1965, Paul VI established that there could be a maximum of 120 "cardinal electors", although in practice both John Paul II and Francis ex-

12. Cfr. Historical notes on the College of Cardinals. Pontifical Yearbook 2013.
13. Ibid.
14. Ibid. Councils are meetings reserved for bishops.
15. Bull "Non mediocri" of Eugene (1439)
16. Constitution Postquam verus, Sixtus V, December 3, 1586.

ceeded that number, and thus provisionally repealed the norm.

It is curious that non-European cardinals were not appointed until 1868.

Who can be appointed cardinals?

The verb used for their appointment is "creation": the pope "creates" new cardinals, since he chooses them freely, regardless of their merits. "The Roman Pontiff freely selects men to be promoted as cardinals, who have been ordained at least into the order of the presbyterate and are especially outstanding in doctrine, morals, piety, and prudence in action; those who are not yet bishops must receive episcopal consecration", recites the 1983 Code of Canon Law[17].

The Code of Canon Law promulgated in 1918 by Benedict XVI had established that cardinals must be priests or bishops and cannot be laymen. In 1962, John XXIII decided that they must always be bishops, a measure that John Paul II confirmed in 1983. In any case, as has happened, popes can dispense from this rule if they deem it appropriate[18].

Is the appointment of cardinal obtained by vote or after some particular studies?

No. It is a title that the pope grants by decree and

17. Cfr. Code of Canon Law, can. 351 § 1
18. For example, in 2020, Pope Francis gave special permission to Cardinal Raniero Cantalamessa so that he would not have to be ordained a bishop and would remain a Capuchin friar.

the fruit of his own, completely personal decision. The Code of Canon Law only specifies that "the Roman Pontiff freely selects men to be promoted as cardinals, who have been ordained at least into the order of the presbyterate and are especially outstanding in doctrine, morals, piety, and prudence in action"[19]. Whoever receives this appointment becomes "prince of the Church" and is integrated into the "College of Cardinals".

Can a layman be appointed a cardinal?

No. The Code of Canon Law promulgated in 1918 by Benedict XV established that cardinals must be priests or bishops and cannot be laymen. In 1962, John XXIII decided that cardinals must be bishops, a measure that John Paul II confirmed in the 1983 Code of Canon Law.

Occasionally popes have granted a dispensation to priests they had named cardinals so that they would not be ordained bishops.

Since a cardinal must have the conditions to become a bishop of Rome in the short term, it is difficult for the pope to grant the same dispensation to a layman.

Have there been lay cardinals?

Yes, until the 19th century, some people who were

19. Cfr. Code of Canon Law, can. 351 § 1

not priests were appointed cardinals. The reason is that in the first centuries of Christianity, bishops were forbidden to change dioceses, so that only people who were not yet bishops could be elected popes. The candidates were priests, deacons or even laymen. After the election, the elected one was immediately ordained bishop of Rome.

Among the laymen elected pope were Leo VIII (963-965), appointed by order of Emperor Otto I of Germany.

The Polish king John Casimir (1609-1672) was a layman and was created a cardinal. In 1858, Pope Pius IX appointed as cardinal the Italian lawyer Teodolfo Mertel, who was then a layman but was ordained deacon that same year. The last lay cardinal was Giacomo Antonelli, created cardinal in the consistory of June 11, 1847 and died in 1876. Since then there has been no other lay cardinal.

Can a priest who is not an ordained bishop be a cardinal?

In 1962, John XXIII established that cardinals must be bishops, and the measure was confirmed in the 1983 Code of Canon Law. However, the pope can grant a dispensation, as recently the Capuchin Cardinal Raniero Cantalamessa or the Dominican Timothy Radcliffe. In the last decades Henri de Lubac, Yves Congar, Pietro Pavan, Paolo Dezza, Mikel Koliqi, Alois Grillmeier, Leo Scheffczyk, Avery Dulles, Roberto Tucci, Tomas Spidlik, Albert Vanhoye, Urbano Navarrete Cortes, Umberto Betti, Domenico Bartolucci or Ernest Simoni have also been dispensed.

The condition is that, if elected pope, they should be able to be ordained bishop immediately.

Who elects the cardinals?

They are chosen solely and exclusively by the Pope.

Do cardinals need special ordination?

No, they do not need a special ordination, since being named a cardinal is not a sacrament. There is a special ceremony of "cardinal creation" called "consistory" in which they receive the parchment with the title of the church of Rome that the pope entrusts to them, and the ring and the red biretta. If they are unable to attend, they are given to them by the nuncio.

What is a consistory?

The word "consistory" derives from the Latin expression "cum sistere", meaning to erect, to make something stand. A consistory is a meeting of the pope with his cardinals. They are summoned by the pontiff to assist him collegially in making decisions on a particular matter[20]. There are two types of consistories, ordinary and extraordinary.

In the ordinary consistory "all the cardinals, at least those present in Rome, are called together to be consulted concerning certain grave matters which occur rather frequently or to carry out certain very solemn

20. Cfr. Code of Canon Law, canon. 353 § 1

acts"[21]. This is the case of a consistory to set a date for canonization. Benedict XVI communicated his resignation during an ordinary consistory.

The extraordinary Consistory is given when the pope convokes all the cardinals, when "particular needs of the Church or the treatment of more grave affairs suggests it"[22]; for example, Francis convoked one in 2014 to prepare for the Synod on the family.

How do the cardinals exercise their role as advisors to the pope?

They do so in three ways: collegially when they participate in the consistories convoked by the pope; when they fulfill their mission as members of dicasteries of the Vatican Curia; or personally, when the pontiff asks for their help.

Are the consistories open to the public?

In general, extraordinary consistories are held behind closed doors. The public may enter only if the pope explicitly permits it in the convocation. For example, ordinary consistories for the creation of new cardinals are public.

What is the ceremony for the creation of cardinals like?

This is an "ordinary consistory", usually held in the Vatican, either in the square or in St. Peter's Basilica,

21. Cfr. Code of Canon Law, canon. 353 § 2
22. Cfr. Code of Canon Law, canon. 353 § 3

or in the great audience hall, the Paul VI Hall. During the ceremony, the pope pronounces the name of each of the new cardinals. They approach him and receive on their knees the red biretta, the cardinal's ring, and the parchment with which a church in Rome is entrusted to them as "presbyters" or "deacons" of this diocese.

What happens if one of the new cardinals dies before the ceremony?

If one of the new cardinals elected by the pope should die between the announcement of the appointment and the consistory of creation of the new cardinals, he will not be considered a cardinal. This happened in 1988 to the Swiss Hans Urs Von Balthasar, who died two days before the ceremony; in 1998 to the Croatian Josip Uhac, then secretary of the Congregation for the Evangelization of Peoples, who died one month and three days before the consistory; and in 2007 to the Polish Ignacy Ludwik Jez, who died one month and eight days before receiving the biretta.

Why is it said that there are cardinal deacons, presbyters and bishops?

Symbolically, the cardinals are incardinated in the diocese of Rome with the title of "bishops", "presbyters" or "deacons". This division reflects an internal hierarchy within the college of cardinals, which distributes them among these three orders or degrees (episcopal, presbyteral or diaconal). Thus, although technically all cardinals are bishops, only a few are incardinated in the diocese of Rome as bishops. Most belong to the "order" of presbyters or deacons.

The episcopal order, of the so-called "cardinal bishops", corresponds to some cardinals of the Vatican Curia and to the Eastern Patriarchs who are cardinals. The former are "incardinated" in dioceses suffragan or dependent on Rome: Ostia, Albano, Frascati, Palestrina, Porto-Santa Rufina, Sabina-Poggio Mirteto and Velletri Segni. The patriarchs, because they preside over an Eastern Rite Church, do not need to be incardinated. The dean of the College of Cardinals is elected from among the members of the group of "cardinal bishops".

Cardinals of the presbyteral order or "presbyteral cardinals" are bishops of dioceses outside Rome, incardinated in parishes of the Eternal City.

Cardinals of the diaconal order or "cardinal deacons" are cardinals of the Curia who receive the "diaconia" of a church in Rome.

In what orders is the College of Cardinals divided?

The cardinals are the image of the clergy of Rome, who had the power to elect the new Pope. Symbolically, when appointing new cardinals, the Pope incardinates these ecclesiastics in the diocese of Rome and entrusts them with a church in this city. According to the type of mission entrusted to them, the college of cardinals is divided into three orders (episcopal, presbyteral and diaconal)[23]. The pope decides to which order each one belongs, following some general rules.

The episcopal order is the most prestigious and

23. Cfr. Code of Canon Law, canon. 350

therefore the cardinal dean is chosen from among its members. It corresponds only to some cardinals of the Vatican Curia specially appointed by the pope, and to the eastern patriarchs who have been made cardinals. They are not entrusted with a church but with one of the suffragan dioceses of Rome: Ostia, Albano, Frascati, Palestrina, Porto-Santa Rufina, Sabina-Poggio Mirteto and Velletri Segni. Patriarchs do not need to be entrusted with any diocese.

Cardinals of the presbyteral order or "cardinal presbyters" are usually bishops of dioceses outside Rome. They are symbolically entrusted with a parish in the city of Rome.

Cardinals of the diaconal order or "cardinal deacons" are cardinals of the Curia who receive the "diaconia" of a church in Rome. Since they already live in Rome, they must only "collaborate" with that church.

When a consistory is convoked, the pope can approve the passage of a cardinal to the higher order, which is done without losing "priority of order and promotion"[24]. In the case of cardinal deacons, "after a full decade in this order, they can accede to the presbyteral order"[25].

What is a cardinal "in pectore"?

This is a cardinal whose identity is known only to the pope and is therefore reserved "in his heart". It refers to cases in which the pontiff prefers not to reveal the identity of the new cardinal, for reasons of security, prudence or personal character. If the pontiff dies without revealing his name, the appointment

24. Cfr. Code of Canon Law, can. 350 § 5 y 6
25. Ibid.

is not valid.

Operationally, "when the Roman Pontiff has announced the selection of a person to the dignity of cardinal but reserves the name of the person in pectore, the one promoted is not bound in the meantime by any of the duties of cardinals nor does he possess any of their rights. After the Roman Pontiff has made his name public, however, he is bound by the same duties and possesses the same rights; he possesses the right of precedence, though, from the day of reservation in pectore"[26].

The first cardinal "in pectore" was Prospero Colonna, secretly named cardinal in 1426 by his uncle Martin V, who did not reveal the name because the cardinal was then only 16 years old. Gregory XVI, in 1845, convoked two consistories, both for a total of five cardinals "in pectore", but never revealed their names and they did not come into effect.

In the 20th century, Paul VI created three cardinals "in pectore": on April 28, 1969, the Czechoslovakian Štěpán Trochta and the Romanian Iuliu Hossu, (he revealed the names on March 5, 1973, when the latter had already died); and on May 24, 1976, František Tomášek, also a Czechoslovakian, whose identity he made public on June 27, 1977.

John Paul II appointed four cardinals "in pectore". These were bishops who were in prison because of their governments' repression of religion. The first was Ignatius Kung Pin-mei, Bishop of Shanghai, whom he created a cardinal in 1979, but did not reveal his name until 1991.

On February 21, 1998, John Paul II appointed 22

26. Cfr. Code of Canon Law, canon. 351 § 3

new cardinals, and among them, two were "in pectore". He made their identities known years later, in the consistory of 2001. They were Marian Jaworski (Ukraine) and Janis Pujats (Latvia).

In the eighth and last consistory convoked by John Paul II, on October 21, 2003, he named 31 new cardinals, of whom one was "in pectore". In this case, the pope died without revealing his name.

Benedict XVI and Francis did not appoint any cardinals "in pectore".

Does only the pope know the cardinals "in pectore"

In principle, only the pope knows their identities.

What is the "College of Cardinals"?

As the Code of Canon Law explains, "the cardinals of the Holy Roman Church constitute a special college which provides for the election of the Roman Pontiff according to the norm of special law"[27]. The meaning of "college" refers to the way they make decisions, which underlines their joint or "collegial" responsibility. Both as a group and personally, when requested, they assist the Pope "especially in the daily care of the universal Church"[28]. "The cardinals especially assist the supreme pastor of the Church through collegial action in consistories in which they are gathered by order of the Roman Pontiff who presides", adds the norm[29]. .They also " are obliged to cooperate assidu-

27. Cfr. Code of Canon Law, canon 349
28. Ibid.
29. Cfr. Code of Canon Law, canon. 353 § 1

ously with the Roman Pontiff"[30].

How many cardinals make up the College of Cardinals?

The number has varied throughout history and has been progressively increasing in recent years. During the High Middle Ages there used to be between twenty and forty. The Councils of Constance (1414-1418) and Basel (1431-1437) limited the number to 24. Under Pius IV (1559-65) the number reached 76, and Sixtus V (1585-1590) fixed the maximum number again at 70 with the Constitution 'Postquam verus' of December 1586, to evoke the 70 elders of Israel chosen by Moses during the Exodus. In practice, in 1958 John XXIII exceeded that number.

The total number of cardinals became irrelevant as of November 21, 1970, when Paul VI established with the motu proprio "Ingravescentem Aetatem" ("Advanced Age") that when a cardinal reaches 80 years of age he loses the right to vote in a conclave. Also Paul VI, in 1975, with the apostolic constitution "Romano Pontifici Eligendo" established that the maximum number of cardinal electors with the right to enter a conclave is 120. In 1996 John Paul II, confirmed this provision in the apostolic constitution "Universi Dominici Gregis" [31].

Since then, popes have tried to ensure that there are always around 120 cardinal electors, under the age of 80, and to ensure this they have on occasion convened consistories with which they have exceeded 120. On February 21, 2001, John Paul II reached 135 cardinal electors. After the consistory of Pope Francis

30. Cfr. Code of Canon Law, canon. 356
31. Cfr. Apostolic Constitution Universi Dominici Gregis (February 22, 1996) Introduction and n. 33.

on December 7, 2024, the college of cardinals reached 253 members, 140 with the right to vote. Never before had there been so many cardinals.[32].

Which popes have created the most cardinals?

John Paul II is the pontiff who created the largest number of cardinals in history: 231 (from 69 nations) in 9 consistories.

Leo XIII (1878-1903) convoked 27 consistories in which he created 147 cardinals.

Pius X (1903-1914) convoked 7 consistories in which he created 50 cardinals.

Benedict XV (1914-1922) convoked 5 consistories in which he created 32 cardinals.

Pius XI (1922-1939) convoked 17 consistories in which he created 76 cardinals.

Pius XII (1939-1958) convoked 2 consistories in which he created 56 cardinals.

John XXIII (1958-1963) convoked 5 consistories in which he created 52 cardinals.

Paul VI (1963-1978) convoked 6 consistories in which he created 143 cardinals.

John Paul I (1978) did not convoke any consistory.

John Paul II (1978-2005) convoked 9 consistories in which he created 231 cardinals.

32. After the consistory of December 7, 2024, the College of Cardinals reached the number of 140 cardinal electors and 113 cardinals over 80 years of age.

Benedict XVI (2005-2013) convened 5 consistories in which he created 90 cardinals.

Francis, until December 7, 2024, convened 10 consistories in which he created 162 cardinals.

At what age should cardinals retire?

The appointment of cardinal is for life. However, according to Paul VI's motu proprio, "Ingravescentem Aetatem" ("Advanced Age"), dated November 21, 1970, when they reach the age of 80, cardinals lose their right to participate in a conclave. If they wish, they can participate in the preparatory meetings prior to the papal election, in which the profile of the next pontiff is defined, but they can neither vote nor enter the conclave.

At that age they also cease to be members of the congregations of the Roman Curia and of the governing bodies of the Holy See. Furthermore, as the Code of Canon Law states, "the cardinals who preside over dicasteries and other permanent institutes of the Roman Curia and Vatican City and who have completed the seventy-fifth year of age are asked to submit their resignation from office to the Roman Pontiff who will see to the matter after considering the circumstances"[33]. Cardinals' offices can be extended until the age of 80.

33. Cfr. Code of Canon Law, canon. 354

Can a cardinal be defrocked?

The pope can expel a cardinal or withdraw the rights and duties attached to this status. Francis expelled U.S. Cardinal Theodore Edgar McCarrick in 2018 after he was shown to have abused minors.

On September 24, 2020, he asked Cardinal Angelo Becciu to renounce his rights and prerogatives as a cardinal, when he was implicated in a case of corruption for the management of Vatican reserved funds. In 2024 he was condemned in the first instance, but he has always maintained his innocence. He did not cease to be a cardinal but renounced the practical consequences of this position.

Can a cardinal resign?

Yes, he can. The first cardinal whose resignation is recorded was Marino Carafa di Belvedere, son of the prince of Belvedere. As he was the second son, following tradition, he pursued an ecclesiastical career. In 1801, when he was 31 years old, Pius VII made him a cardinal. Six years later, in 1807, the pontiff allowed him to renounce the cardinalate, so that he could ensure the descendants of his family. He married the noblewoman Marianna Gaetani dell'Aquila and they had two children.

In 1837, Carlo Odescalchi, Cardinal Vicar of Rome, presented to Pope Gregory XVI the resignation of all his offices to become a Jesuit. The pope did not accept. A year later, in 1838, he granted him this permission.

In 1927, the Frenchman Louis Billot resigned from the cardinalate and gave Pope Pius XI his scarlet biretta, his ring and his pectoral cross in protest to the Pope's rejection of the traditionalist Catholic association "Action française". Pius XI accepted his resignation eight days later.

In March 2013, during the Sede Vacante following the resignation of Benedict XVI, the dean of the College of Cardinals announced that the Scotsman Keith O'Brien was resigning from participating in the conclave, due to his sexual misconduct with young adults. In 2015 he definitively renounced his rights and duties as a cardinal

On September 24, 2020, Giovanni Angelo Becciu renounced his cardinal rights and prerogatives when he was implicated in a corruption case involving the management of Vatican funds. He was condemned in the first instance but has always maintained his innocence.

What are the signs or insignia of the cardinals?

The color of the cardinals is scarlet, which evokes their promise to give their lives to the service of the Church and the successor of Peter. Among their insignia, the following could be highlighted:

1) The cardinal's "cappello".

It is a scarlet red hat with a wide brim. Currently in disuse, it is only present on the coat of arms of the cardinals. In ancient times it was the sign worn by freed slaves and was used by free citizens on feasts and solemnities. It signifies the glorious freedom that Christians have received. This garment appears in the decree of the first Council of Lyon, in 1245, which establishes the dress of cardinals. Nowadays in consistories they use the "biretta", which is a hat with three peakss.

2) The cardinal's ring.

It is worn by all the bishops, to remind them of their betrothal to their diocesan Church, where they act as Christ the Bridegroom. The cardinals receive it from the hands of the Pope as a sign of their betrothal to the Church of Rome and, therefore, to the whole Universal Church.

3) Footwear

There were rules on the footwear of cardinals in a document entitled "Norme Ceremoniali per gli Eminentissimmi Cardinali", "Norms for the Cardinals' Ceremonies". This text has fallen into disuse and cardinals now wear black men's shoes, with the only stipulation that they not be conspicuous.

What is the meaning of the scarlet color in which the cardinals wear?

Red is the color of the emperors' vestments, and according to tradition, Constantine gave it to the pontiff as recognition of his authority. The pope allowed the use of this color to his main collaborators, also as a sign that they participated in his authority and mission. Progressively, its use was limited to the cardinals[34].

The scarlet color symbolizes the commitment of the cardinals to defend the Church to the shedding of their blood and to pay with death if necessary. At the Council of Lyon (1245), Pope Innocent IV introduced the scarlet hat as proper to the garb of the cardinals and explained that this color indicates that they are

34. Cfr. "The Pope is dead, long live the Pope", José Apeles Santolaria de Puey y Cruells. Barcelona, 1997

"always ready to shed blood for the defense of the faith". That same pontiff told the cardinals on another occasion that with the scarlet biretta "he wanted to remind them that they should be ready at all times to shed blood for the protection of the freedom of the Christian people"[35].

What is the significance of the hat worn by cardinals?

Pope John XXIII explained that "the cardinal's biretta is the contracted form of a precious veil, with which the noblest part of the human constitution is enveloped. It is the seat of good ideas, of generous intentions, of the highest and purest spiritual elevations. As far as physical health itself is concerned, what matters most is the head, preserved, even in old age, robust, healthy and serene"[36].

Which pope introduced the use of the scarlet biretta for cardinals?

This was done by Pope Paul II (1464-1471), to give them a sign that would distinguish them from other prelates in solemn ceremonies.

Which is the most important cardinal?

Technically, the most important is the cardinal dean, followed by the vice-dean. Both preside over

35. De Historia Francorum, Parisiis 1708, Lib. VII fol. 112.
36. John XXIII's address to Cardinal Giovanni Battista Montini, the first of the new cardinals, on the meaning of the biretta. December 17, 1958

the college of cardinals "as equals". He must reside in Rome. The Code of Canon Law clarifies that "Neither the dean nor the assistant dean possesses any power of governance over the other cardinals but is considered as first among equals"[37].

The Cardinal Camerlengo also has particular functions, although these are limited only to the period of the Sede Vacante.

What are the functions of the Dean of the College of Cardinals?

Apart from the specific functions during a period of Sede Vacante, such as presiding at the pope's funeral and also at the conclave if he is less than 80 years old, his usual function is to exercise a "fraternal" presidency. It falls to him, for example, to celebrate the funeral of cardinals who die, to convoke the cardinals for consistories, to communicate to the cardinals certain dispositions of the pope, or to pronounce speeches or declarations on behalf of the cardinals. According to tradition, in the hierarchy of cardinals, "the cardinal dean holds as his title the Diocese of Ostia together with the other church he already has as a title"[38].

How is the cardinal dean appointed?

He is elected by a vote of the cardinals of the order of bishops and the pope confirms the appointment,

37. Cfr. Code of Canon Law, can. 352 § 1
38. Cfr. Code of Canon Law, can. 350 § 4

which lasts a maximum of five years.

Who is the "Cardinal Camerlengo"?

He is the cardinal who during the Sede Vacante represents the head of state of the Vatican City State and defends the temporal interests of the Holy See. He must always give an account of his decisions to the College of Cardinals. Outside the Sede Vacante, the cardinal Camerlengo has no specific function.

Who is the Pope

What does the word "pope" mean?

The word comes from the Greek πάππας "popes", which also means "priest" and bishop", and is attributed to these religious ministries because they are considered "fathers in the faith". From the eleventh century in the West the title was reserved to the bishop of Rome.

There are interpretations that want to derive this word from the first letters of the phrase "Petri Apostoli Potestatem Accipiens", "he who receives authority from the apostle Peter"; or from the union of the first letters of the Latin words "Pater Pastor", "father and shepherd".

What is the mission of the Popes?

The "Brief Dictionary of the Popes", by Tomás Álvarez, says that principally "his mission is to be the vicar of Jesus on earth and in the history of mankind"[39]. As the definition contained in this dictionary adds, it also corresponds to him to be "propagator and servant of his Gospel" and "to preside within the Church over the activity of the successors of the

39. ALVAREZ Tomás, Diccionario breve de los Papas: De San Pedro a Benedicto XVI, Editorial Monte Carmelo, Burgos, 2005, p. 11

apostles that exist in the whole world", in reference to the patriarchs, bishops, presbyters, and, for example, missionaries

He explains that in the Catholic tradition, the pope is assigned a triple service pertaining to: doctrine, sanctification and government.

Doctrinal service means being a teacher of the Gospel truth and, when necessary, to clarify it even with an "ex cathedra" definition. This service of the truth has imposed on the popes very serious sacrifices, including martyrdom.

The second is the service of "sanctification" through the sacraments, especially the sacrament of Holy Orders, since all priests, bishops and patriarchs exercise their sacramental mission in communion with the pope. Moreover, it is up to him to recognize the sanctity of those who have heroically lived the Gospel ideal, for it is he who canonizes the new saints.

As for the service of government, it reminds us that "the Church is not only the mystical body of Jesus, but also the pilgrim people of God and a society of humans that needs to be presided over and governed by the Vicar of Jesus. For this reason, the Pope not only presides over the councils, but his authority is over them and over the episcopal colleges of the various nations," concludes this dictionary.

What titles does the pope receive?

According to the Annuario Pontificio, the Pope, in addition to "Bishop of Rome", receives these historical titles: "Vicar of Christ, Successor of the Prince of the Apostles, Supreme Pontiff of the Universal Church,

Patriarch of the West, Primate of Italy, Archbishop and Metropolitan of the Roman Province, Sovereign of the City State of the Vatican City State, Servant of the Servants of God".

Is the pope a saint?

The title given to him by calling him "Holy Father" is not equivalent to being canonized during his lifetime, but rather an expression of affection on the part of the people, which also reminds him of the great responsibility that rests on his shoulders.

The pontiff, like any baptized person, is "*called*" to holiness, for this is the invitation of Sacred Scripture: "As he who called you is holy, so you also must be holy in all your conduct, for it is written, 'You shall be holy, for I am holy'"[40].

The path to holiness, which the Catholic Church understands not as perfection or impeccability but as love of God manifested in the form of loving consistency with one's faith, begins with the sacrament of baptism and continues throughout life. To attain it, God's help and grace are not enough. It is also necessary to strive to live according to God's plan and to do works of mercy.

The path can mean going forward or going backward because every human being has the daily possibility of choosing between good and evil. Whoever is considered the worst of sinners can be converted and become a great saint and, also, whoever seems to be a saint can become the worst of sinners. For this reason, a person can only be recognized as a saint after his death.

40. 1 Peter 1, 15-16

The Catholic Church initiates the process of canonization or official declaration of sainthood, in the case of certain persons who may be exemplary. In order to carry it ahead, an investigation is done and testimonies are gathered to prove with concrete facts that he or she lived the faith in a heroic way. It also includes the request that God ratify this reputation for sanctity with a miracle.

The Pope has the responsibility to personally seek holiness and, moreover, to be an example to the people, but, as chosen by Christ and a fundamental part of the Church, he can also be tempted by the devil to make him fall. In fact, this happened to St. Peter, the first Vicar of Christ. For this reason, the Church always prays for him, so that God may protect, help and enlighten him.

What has the papacy been like in history?

The history of each pope can be considered from different points of view: the biographical aspect, his pastoral or doctrinal work, the political aspect, his support for the arts, etc. The "History of the Popes", written by the Austrian Ludwig von Pastor, published in several volumes, is recommended[41].

The "Brief Dictionary of the Popes" recalls that in the first centuries of Christianity, many popes "were victims of the imperial persecutions of Rome" or "martyrs"[42]. Later they became a political power and had to face the interference of emperors from Byz-

41. The work begins in 1417 and ends in 1799. He published the first volume in 1886. Until 1926 he published another twelve volumes. Volume XIII is from 1928. The rest of the volumes are posthumous, since the author died in 1928. Volume XIV was published in 1929-30; volume XV in 1931; and volume XVI in 1932-33.
42. Cfr. ALVAREZ Tomás, Diccionario breve de los Papas: De San Pedro a Benedicto XVI, Editorial Monte Carmelo, Burgos, 2005

antium and the Germanic Empire. This is also the period in which the first great schisms occurred. From the 10th century, their territorial power increased, but also the pressures from noble families of Rome, from the kings of the Catholic powers, such as France, Spain or Germany, and from the popular revolts. In modern history, Napoleon and the Piedmontese army humiliated the pope. Since 1929, the papacy ceases to be a territorial power, to focus on spiritual leadership. Since then, governments put pressure on the pope with other mechanisms, without the need to invade his territory.

How many popes have existed to date?

From St. Peter to Pope Francis there have been 266 popes. This means that Francis is the 265th successor of St. Peter.

Has there ever been a woman pope?

No. The story about the closeness of a woman to Pope John VIII (IX century) was distorted and collected in the XIII century by Martin of Opava in his "Chronicon pontificum et imperatorum". It is the story of "the Papisa Juana", which spread in the XVI century by some Protestant sectors with the intention of discrediting the papacy. It relates that a woman pretended to be a man and became bishop of Rome. During a procession the supposed papisa fell to the ground and began to give birth, so that the people discovered the deception and murdered her.

Why don't popes use their first name and instead give themselves another name?

The change of name refers to a biblical tradition by which some Old Testament characters received a new name linked to the beginning of a special vocation. This is the case of Abraham, Jacob or the apostle Peter, who was originally called Simon. The first pope to change his name was Mercurio di Proietto, who as pope was called John II and ruled the Church from 533 to 535.

Since when do popes change their name when elected?

The first to do so was John II (533-535), because he was called Mercury, the name of a pagan divinity, and he thought it convenient to have a Christian name.

It happened again centuries later, when in 955 Octavian Alberic of the Counts of Tusculum decided to use the name John XII for papal decisions and Octavian for his private decisions. Since then, it was changed by all but two popes. In 1522, Adrian VI kept the name, as did Marcellus II in 1555.

In 1009, Pietro Boccapecora was elected pope. He preferred to change his name to Sergius so as not to keep the name of the first apostle. In 1261, Pope Urban IV began the custom of including the ordinal number after his name, to differentiate himself from his predecessors. In 1978 John Paul I became the first pontiff to choose a compound name.

What is the most common name used by pontiffs?

The most commonly used name so far is John. There have been 25 pontiffs who have chosen it, including John Paul I and John Paul II.

Why is he called the Supreme Pontiff?

It is the only title of the Roman Empire still in force. The expression derives from the Latin, "pontifex maximus", "chief bridge builder", the most important religious title during Imperial Rome. It is linked to the construction of one of the oldest bridges on the Tiber, which was made of wood and built in the 7th century BC.

After Emperor Augustus, from 12 B.C., "pontifex maximus" became one of the titles of the emperors. In 376, the emperor Gratian, a Christian, renounced this title and gave it to the bishop of Rome.

"Pontifex" means "bridge builder". With this title we are reminded that the Pope is the Vicar or representative of Christ on earth and with his work he brings God closer to mankind and mankind closer to God.

What are the signs or insignia of the pope?

In addition to the characteristic symbols of bishops, which are the miter, crosier and episcopal ring, the pope has other signs or insignia to communicate his authority or to underline elements of his spirituality. It could be said that the signs or insignia of the pope are the following:

White cassock with white capelet.

The fisherman's ring

The pallium

The pectoral cross

The pastoral staff

White skullcap

There are some other distinctive symbols of the papacy that have ceased to be used, such as the papal tiara, the camauro, the papal throne, the gestational chair, the gonfalon, the flabella, the phanon, the asterisk, the fistula.

How do you recognize the pope?

The pope wears a white cassock with a white "muceta" or capelet. The "esclavina" is a short cape that covers the shoulders and is fastened at the front. This white vestment can only be worn by the pope, which is why Benedict XVI stopped wearing it when he became pope emeritus. On solemn occasions, such as the papal election, the cape is red.

How does the pope's cassock differ from that worn by other priests?

Generally all priests wear black cassocks, although those from hot countries may also wear white. Bishops or archbishops wear black cassocks with purple edges or, also, on solemn occasions, purple cassocks.

Cardinals wear black cassocks with a scarlet sash and buttons, or only a scarlet cassock.

Since when does the pope wear white?

For the pope to use the color white, it was necessary to have a Dominican pontiff, a religious order whose members always dress like this. There have been five Dominican successors to St. Peter: Innocent V, who was pope for six months in 1276; Benedict XI from 1302 to 1304; Nicholas V from 1447 to 1455; Pius V from 1566 to 1572, and Benedict XIII from 1724 to 1730.

The first three kept the white habit of their order, because they wanted to maintain their link with that spirituality. However, when they died, their successor dressed like any other bishop. From the time of the Dominican Pius V (1566-1572), the white vestment of the popes became generalized. After him, his successors, even if they were no longer Dominicans, continued to dress like this.

In addition to consolidating the custom of popes wearing white, Pius V went down in history for commissioning the painter Daniele da Volterra to "dress" the figures that Michelangelo had painted nude in the Last Judgment in the Sistine Chapel. Also, by means of the bull "*De Salutis Gregis Dominici*" of November 1, 1567, he prohibited attending bullfights under penalty of excommunication: for the pontiff it was nonsense for a person to endanger his own life to offer a spectacle.

Who makes the Pope's cassock?

In Rome there are two great tailors who traditionally deal with papal cassocks, Gammarelli and Mancinelli. The Gammarelli house has been dressing popes and cardinals for 250 years. It is a tailor's shop located in the heart of Rome, in Piazza della Minerva. Its shop window always displays liturgical vestments for pontiffs and cardinals, such as cassocks, skullcaps and even scarlet socks.

Another Roman tailor is Raniero Mancinelli, who has his workshop in the Borgo district, very close to the Vatican. It is said that he was the one who prepared Benedict XVI's cassocks. When asked how much the pope's suit cost, the tailor replied, "Unfortunately I have forgotten."

What is the meaning of the white skullcap or zucchetto worn by the pope?

It was born for practical use and became over time a sign of dignity. The skullcap, also known as "zucchetto", "papalina", "pileolo" or "pileolus" is a small round and concave cap made of eight segments worn by bishops and the pope as a sign of sacredness and authority.

Since during the rite of consecration of the Mass and even after communion it is removed because Christ is physically present in the Eucharist, it is called "solideo", because "soli Deo tollitur" (only before God is it removed).

It is similar to the "kippah" that practicing Jews use as a symbol of humility of the human creature before God. They consider it evoking the episode of the Tower of Babel, so that it marks the boundary between Heaven and earth and helps them not to transgress the limits of Heaven, God's dwelling place. It also recalls "the hand of God" that offers protection.

The bishops and cardinals take it off before the Roman Pontiff in recognition that he is the Vicar of Christ. Benedict XVI also removed it when he greeted Pope Francis.

The white color is reserved for the Pope. The abbots and priests can use it in black. The canons and monsignors use it with purple or crimson borders (red and light tonality), according to their degree. Bishops wear a purple one; apostolic nuncios representing the Holy See, purple; some archbishops, because they are primates or have some special offices, may also wear crimson. Cardinals and some distinguished archbishops wear scarlet, such as the Patriarch of Venice, and the archbishops of Salzburg and Vercelli.

The biretta and the miter can be placed on top of the skullcap.

What does the fisherman's ring symbolize?

It is a symbol of papal government, since in ancient times it was used as a seal that guaranteed that the pope had reviewed and approved a certain document. Now, for convenience, the pope's decisions are certified with a special stamp and not with his ring[43].

Each new pope receives this ring from the hands of the senior cardinal before the beginning of the Mass for the inauguration of his pontificate. Thereafter, he

43. Cfr. PYKE, Edgar Royston (2001). Dictionary of Religions. Trad. Elsa Cecilia Frost (2nd edition). Fondo de Cultura Económica. Mexico. pp. 359. Voice: *Anillo*

wears it on his right ring finger on occasions of particular solemnity[44].

The ring is non-transferable, is made specifically for each pontiff and must be destroyed when he dies or resigns so that his decisions are not falsified. The cardinal camerlengo is in charge of annulling it, although the College of Cardinals must verify that he has done so. Usually, the camerlengo simply draws a cross on the relief, so that it is "annulled", but not materially destroyed.

In Latin it is called "*annulus piscatorius*". It has this name because it depicts the first bishop of Rome, the apostle Peter, a fisherman from Galilee, with his boat and nets. It is usually made of gold or silver and is engraved with the name of the pontiff who uses it. The first pope who is known to have worn the "fisherman's ring" is Clement IV, pontiff in the 13th century[45].

What is the pallium?

It is a white woolen band, about five centimeters wide, which is placed around the shoulders and back of the pontiff, and which he gives to the patriarchs and bishops of metropolitan archdioceses as a symbol of communion with the Holy See. It is therefore a "sign of jurisdiction". It represents his authority as a "shepherd" who carries his "sheep" on his shoulders.

It is inspired by a garment of Ancient Greece, inherited by the Roman Empire, and later derived from the toga to become a liturgical garment.

44. Ordo Rituum pro Ministerii Petrini Initio Romae Episcopi.
45. Maurice M. Hasset, Catholic Encyclopedia, Fisherman's Ring (Spanish edition).

Until the pontificate of John Paul II, the pontiffs' pallium was embroidered with six black crosses[46]. Benedict XVI modified the shape of the pallium on two occasions. At the beginning of his pontificate, he returned to the style used before the 10th century, which appears in ancient mosaics, crossed over the shoulder and with five red crosses as a symbol of the passion of Christ. That pallium was very uncomfortable, and he stopped using it. Curiously, on April 28, 2009, he left it as a tribute on the tomb of Celestine V, the last pontiff who had resigned until that point.

Months before, already in June 2008, he had been wearing one similar to that of John Paul II's time, but with red crosses. The idea was to distinguish it from the pallium of the metropolitan archbishops, which has black crosses, "to signify the diversity of jurisdiction".

Francis resumed the use of the pallium with the black crosses, to underline the aspect of unity with the rest of the bishops around the world.

What is the significance of the pectoral cross?

It is a large cross worn around the neck by the pope, cardinals, bishops and abbots. It can be simple or "pontifical". The simple one is usually used, attached to a chain. The pontifical is used in solemn ceremonies and is usually adorned with jewels.

Sometimes it is attached to the cassock with a cord whose color varies according to the dignity of the wearer: for the pope it is gold, for cardinals it is red

46. Cfr. PYKE, Edgar Royston (2001). Dictionary of Religions. Trad. Elsa Cecilia Frost (2nd edition). Fondo de Cultura Económica. Mexico. pp. 359. Voice: *Palio*

with gold, and for archbishops and bishops it is green with gold. This use is infrequent.

Francis opted for a silver cross and avoided using gold pectoral crosses and cords.

What is the crozier used by popes and what does it signify?

The crozier is a staff that each bishop receives during the ceremony of his consecration, as a sign of his pastoral mission. It can be made of very different materials: wood, ivory, iron, bronze, silver or even gold. Some are masterpieces of goldsmithing. Bishops use it during Mass or other solemn offices.

In order to be easily transported and handled, it usually consists of two or three parts. The lower part is straight and is called "palo" or "shaft". The upper part is the most ornamented. It has at its base a spherical or prismatic knot called "staff" or "scroll". The bishops of the Greek rite replace the scroll with an ornamented T-shaped crosspiece and decorate the shaft with artistic knots and other work.

The Pope does not carry a "crozier" but a "pastoral". The difference is that at the top he has a crucifix.

What is the mitre worn by the pope and bishops?

It is a headdress or adornment worn by all bishops at mass, hence these hierarchs are called "mitred" and their jurisdiction is called "mitre". It may also be worn by abbots and prelates. The pope wears it as bishop of Rome.

It consists of two pieces of fabric in the shape of a rhombus, with two parts, one at the front and the other at the back, which end in the shape of a beak at the top. From the back hang two bands of cloth called "infulas" representing the authority of the Old and New Testament.

It is worn over the skullcap, but is used only in liturgical ceremonies, generally during mass. It can vary in color according to the liturgical seasons.

What was the papal tiara?

It was a triple crown worn by the popes, and was also called "triple tiara" or, in Latin, "triregnum". Being a crown, it was made of precious metals and embellished with precious stones. In addition, it was topped by a small cross on a sphere.

Originally the three crowns represented the pope's sovereignty over the Papal States, his spiritual power over civil society, and his papal authority over that of the rest of the civil princes. Today, the Catholic Church professes that the triple tiara symbolizes the three primates of the pontiff: primacy of sacred order, primacy of jurisdiction and primacy of magisterium.

Its use became widespread from the twelfth century onwards. It was used during the coronation at the beginning of the pontificate and the pope wore it on some solemn occasions[47]. The last pontiff to be crowned with a tiara was Paul VI, in 1963. Two years later, after the Second Vatican Council (1965), he gave up wearing it.

47. PYKE, Edgar Royston. Op. cit. Voice: *Tiara*

In 1996, John Paul II officially abolished the term "coronation" and replaced it with "ceremony of inauguration of the pontificate"[48]. Although they had stopped using it, the tiara was still present in the coat of arms of the popes, until in 2005 Benedict XVI decided to replace it with a silver miter with three golden stripes, so that it highlights his religious authority and unity with the rest of the bishops.

What was the camauro?

The name of this garment comes from the Latin "*camelaucum*", and this from the Greek "*kamelauchion*", "camel hair cap". In ancient times it was used by nobles to protect themselves from the cold.

It is red, the color reserved for pontiffs, with a white ermine trim reminiscent of Santa Claus. It could not be worn during liturgical ceremonies, especially the Mass, where it is prescribed that the pope wears a white skullcap and miter. Some pontiffs wore it in winter instead of the biretta, especially when giving the blessing on the balcony of the Vatican Basilica or when going out to St. Peter's Square.

Many Renaissance and Baroque pontiffs were portrayed wearing the camauro. John XXIII wore it on some occasions. It was not worn by Paul VI, John Paul I or John Paul II. Benedict XVI wore it in the popemobile tour prior to the cold general audiences of Dec. 21 and 28, 2005, but it sparked strong criticism because it was considered a restoration of forms of the past, so he did not wear it again. "I was just cold, and I happen to have a sensitive head. And I said, since the camauro is there, then let's put it on. But I was real-

48. Constitución Apostólica Universi Dominici Gregis. Art. 92

ly just trying to fight off the cold. I haven't put it on again since. In order to forestall over-interpretation", Benedict XVI explained[49].

What was the papal throne like?

More than the throne of a king or monarch, it is the chair, seat or cathedra from which the pope presides, governs, teaches and animates the community. In the great Roman basilicas there is a "see" reserved for the pontiff, which is used on solemn occasions.

Pope Francis requested that a chair without golden elements be used for him, like the one used by his guests, to avoid the figure of the successor of Peter being identified with that of a Renaissance monarch.

What is the gestational chair?

It is a chair supported by two crossbeams that allow one to lift and transport a person carrying the seat on one's shoulders. It was used to carry the pope in procession in solemn ceremonies, so that the crowd could see him. Those in charge of carrying it are the "pontifical sediari".

The last pope to be transported in this portable chair was John Paul I, who used it for the three general audiences he held during his short 33-day pontificate in September 1978. Formally it has never been removed but, in practice, in St. Peter's Square it was replaced in the 1980s by the popemobile, while in the audience hall and in the basilica it is possible to see

49. Benedict XVI. Light of the World - The Pope, the Church and the Signs of the Times A Conversation with Peter Seewald, Libreria Editrice Vaticana, 2010

the pontiff thanks to video screens.

John Paul II never used the "gestatorial chair", but the "sediari" did assist him by guiding the mobile pedestal with which he moved while standing during the long processions in the basilica, since Christmas 1999. Also since October 2011, Benedict XVI began to use the same pedestal, pushed by the "sediari" to avoid the fatigue of walking the central nave of St. Peter's covered with heavy vestments.

The gestational chair has provoked many anecdotes in the Vatican. After the pontificate of the thin Pius XII, in 1958 it was the turn of John XXIII, who was more obese. When the "sediari" raised him for the first time, he jokingly promised them that he would raise their salaries because from then on they would have to work twice as hard because he was overweight.

Who are the "pontifical sediari"?

Those responsible for carrying the gestatorial chair were the "pontifical sediari", a position reserved for lay assistants. According to tradition, this task dates back to the second or third century and refers to a group in charge of carrying the "sede" or chair to the places where the successor of Peter would have presided over a ceremony or a meeting. The oldest documents recording its existence date back to the 14th century.

The "college of pontifical sediari" is still in force in the Vatican, although now its function is to coordinate the ceremony of papal audiences and celebrations. They come from families in Rome who have performed this task for centuries, since technically they belong to the "close family of the Pope". They are a select group of lay men, personally appointed by the pope to this lifelong role. They greet visitors at the door of the pope's residence, guide them through the rooms and eventually give them directions on how the meeting will proceed. Also, during the Wednesday general audiences, they are in charge of accompanying people who have asked to greet the pope personally.

Until 1972 they wore a carmine-colored uniform, and until a few years earlier they also wore a hat with two peaks. According to tradition, these ancient uniforms were designed by Raphael. The carmine color evoked the blood of the martyrs on which the boat of Peter rests

They now wear a gray morning coat, almost violet, with pants of the same color, gray vest and white shirt, gloves and bow tie. The morning coat has no buttons, but closes with a chain with a brooch of the keys of Peter, symbol of the Holy See.

It is their responsibility to carry the Pope's coffin.

What was the gonfalon?

The "confalon" or "gonfalon" is an upright standard, banner or flag, suspended from a crossbar and sometimes ending in one or two points. It was used in medieval Italian communes and later by guilds, corporations and local districts. Its design includes insignia, coats of arms or showy ornaments. Its use was later extended to processions and ecclesiastical ceremonies.

It had great importance as a Christian religious object in Europe during the Middle Ages, especially in central Italy. In this case it consisted of a cloth held by a T-shaped wooden frame at the back, and with a long pole to hold the banner in religious ceremonies and processions.

The banners were painted with tempera or oil, sometimes on both sides. They bore images of God the Father, Jesus Christ, the Virgin and Child, or the patron saints of the cities, brotherhoods or guilds. The gonfalon was generally kept in a chapel guarded by a specific brotherhood or religious group. During processions, it was carried by a member of that brotherhood.

Between the 13th and 16th centuries it was traditional to make specific gonfalons for processions in which specific graces were asked to God, such as the end of epidemics.

In the Vatican, this banner was used as an insignia in processions attended by the pontiff. Some papal basilicas have a gonfalon on display, which is opened only when the pope visits.

Now the gonfalon is used only in heraldry, in coats of arms of institutions related to the Holy See, such as that of these basilicas, or the coats of arms of the Sede Vacante, (in which it appears next to the two keys) and that of the cardinal Camerlengo.

What is flabella?

In old photos of papal ceremonies, the presence of enormous feather fans on the pontiff's back is striking. They are called flabellae. Its name comes from the Latin "flabellum" (fan), which derives from "flabrum", "breath of wind". They are giant fans that are handled with a pole, made with large ostrich or peacock feathers.

In ancient times, for example in Egypt, Mesopotamia and Rome, they were used as a royal and religious insignia. They were also used to fan the flame on altars and even to scare away insects, provide shade and cool the environment.

They began to be used in papal Masses to ward off insects attracted by the flames and the wine. It is mentioned in the "Apostolic Constitutions", a work of the fourth century erroneously attributed to the apostles that collects some elements of liturgical and disciplinary nature: "*Let two of the deacons, on each side of the altar, keep a fan, formed of thin membranes, or by feathers of the peacock, or by fine fabrics and in silence, drive away the small animals that fly, so that they can not approach the cups*"[50].

When the communion of the faithful under the two species (bread and wine) in the Latin rite Mass was suppressed in the 14th century, the flabella was no longer necessary. From then on they were used in an ornamental way. They were carried in pairs by the "flabelliferae". Once the pope reached his throne, they were placed on each side of it, one or two steps behind. Paul VI abolished this practice in the 1960s.

The Orthodox and Eastern Catholic Churches use the "*ripidion*", which is a round metal or wooden fan, engraved or painted with the image of a six-winged seraphim. The rod that holds it is a little longer than that of the Latin flabella.

50. Cited in Catholic Encyclopedia, New York. Robert Appleton Company, 1913.

What was the fanon?

The "fanon" is a kind of closed cape that falls over the shoulders and chest, and that the pontiff can wear in solemn masses over the liturgical vestments. It symbolizes the shield of faith that protects the Catholic Church, represented by the pope. Although it was not expressly abolished with the liturgical reform following the Second Vatican Council, it did fall into disuse.

Paul VI used it for the last time in 1964; John Paul I never used it; John Paul II used it only once, at the beginning of his pontificate, in the Basilica of St. Cecilia in Rome. Benedict XVI incorporated it back into the papal liturgy in 2012, and wore it at three Masses, the last one on January 6, 2013, a few days before announcing his resignation. Since then, it has not been used again.

What is the "asterisk" in the papal liturgy?

Its name comes from the Greek ἀστερίσκον, "*asteriskon*", star, as in religious ceremonies it recalls the star of Bethlehem. It is a liturgical object of precious metal created so that the veil covering the paten does not touch the consecrated Host - the paten is the metal saucer where the Host is placed in the liturgy. It is still used for the same purpose in the Eucharist of the Orthodox and Greek Catholic Churches.

In the past, it was used in the Latin Rite Church during papal ceremonies. In this case, it has twelve arms, each of which recalls an apostle. Benedict XVI used it on occasion.

What was "fistula", in the papal liturgy?

It was a golden cannula used only by the pope to take communion under the species of wine. During the papal ceremonies, the pontiff did not usually receive communion on the altar, as he does nowadays, but a little apart, on the cathedra. For this reason, the consecrated host and a large chalice were brought close to him. To avoid spilling it, he drank through that cannula of precious metal.

Since the liturgical reform implemented after the Second Vatican Council, the pope directly communes the consecrated wine from the chalice and this object is no longer necessary.

Does the pope wear special footwear?

The short answer is no. John Paul II wore dark shoes at the beginning of his pontificate. Benedict respected the tradition of wearing red shoes. Francis wears black, orthopedic shoes.

The truth is that there is a special shoe that is reserved for the pope, but that has fallen into disuse. They were red. Some authors believe that it represents his authority, the power in Heaven and earth conferred by Christ to Peter and his successors, the tongues of fire of the Holy Spirit, his disposition to martyrdom, etc. It was the color reserved for Byzantine emperors

Until now, during the conclave, in the sacristy of the Sistine Chapel there are several pairs of red shoes of different sizes ready for the new pontiff to put on as soon as he is elected, and to wear during his first public appearance from the balcony of St. Peter's Basilica.

Before the liturgical reform made by Pius X in 1911, at Mass the popes wore shoes of the same color as the vestments. White was reserved for feast days or solemnities; red, in memory of the martyrs and on Palm Sunday, Good Friday and Pentecost; purple, in penitential time, that is, Advent and Lent; green, on days of Ordinary Time. Thus, the pope changed the color of his shoes according to the color of the vestments and the shoes and the chasuble had the same color.

As a general rule, the shoes worn by the Pope do not usually have flashy ornaments and avoid shiny patent leather. Francis buys them at an orthopedic shop near the Vatican, in Via del Gelsomino. When Benedict XVI retired, he stopped wearing red shoes and put on those given to him by shoemakers in Leon, Guanajuato (Mexico), which were much more comfortable.

In the recent past, several shoemakers have claimed to make shoes for the pope. One of them is Danilo Mancini, who works for the firm Gammarelli, specialized in religious attire, and has his workshop in Rome, in Vicolo della Volpe. Also Gianfranco Pittarel, based in Via Masserano, Turin, made some shoes for John XXIII, Paul VI and some for John Paul II. Another is Adriano Stefanelli, who has his workshop in Via Cavour, Rome. He has made shoes for John Paul II and Benedict XVI. The shoes have a label inside with the name of his father, Antonio Stefanelli, as a tribute to his teachings. Peruvian shoemaker Antonio Arellano repaired shoes for John Paul II and Benedict XVI in his workshop in Via del Falco, near the Vatican.

Does the Pope go to confession?

Pope Francis said that he used to go to confession every two weeks. Benedict XVI also spoke of his confessor when he died. And the fact is that, like all human beings, popes are exposed to falling into sin and need the help of the sacrament of reconciliation. In any case, the pope must also fulfill the precept of going to confession at least once a year, and when he commits a grave or mortal sin.

Each pontiff chooses his own confessor and spiritual director.

Is the pope infallible, or can he be wrong?

Papal infallibility is real, but it is limited to very few questions or definitions, on which he has asked for special help and advice before pronouncing on it himself. It was defined as "dogma of" faith at the First Vatican Council, inaugurated on December 8, 1869, as a response to liberalism and rationalism, which disregarded the transcendent conception of the person. On July 18, 1870, the apostolic constitution "Pastor Aeternus" was approved, which determined that when the Pope spoke "ex cathedra" on questions of faith and morals, he was infallible. Theologically it is based on the promise that Jesus makes to Peter that he will have special assistance.

It means that the Pope is infallible only when he pronounces himself as "pastor of the universal Church" and not as a private person, and intervenes with "a definitive act to proclaim a doctrine concerning faith and morals". Since it was proclaimed in 1870, this prerogative has been put into practice only once, in 1950, when Pius XII proclaimed the dogma of the

Assumption of the Virgin Mary into Heaven.

The Pope, like any other person, can have errors of vision, calculation, appreciation, etc. And also, like any person, he has the possibility to correct and amend them. The first pope, Peter made a mistake when he denied Christ three times, but he corrected his mistake when he accepted Him again as his Lord.

Is it true that the pope is the "antichrist"?

To answer this question, it is worth quoting the words of the Apostle John in his two epistles: "Who is the liar? Whoever denies that Jesus is the Christ. Whoever denies the Father and the Son, this is the antichrist"[51]. "Many deceivers have gone out into the world, those who do not acknowledge Jesus Christ as coming in the flesh; such is the deceitful one and the antichrist"[52].

Matthew's Gospel also states: "False messiahs and false prophets will arise, and they will perform signs and wonders so great as to deceive, if that were possible, even the elect"[53].

And St. Paul also agrees: "Now the Spirit explicitly says that in the last times some will turn away from the faith by paying attention to deceitful spirits and demonic instructions"[54]. "Let no one deceive you in any way. For unless the apostasy comes first and the lawless one is revealed, - the one doomed to perdition, who opposes and exalts himself above every so-called god and object of worship, so as to seat himself

51. 1 John 2, 22
52. 2 John 1, 7
53. Matthew 24, 24
54. 1 Timothy 4,1

in the temple of God, - claiming that he is a god -. (...) And then the lawless one will be revealed, whom the Lord [Jesus] will kill with the breath of his mouth and render powerless by the manifestation of his coming"[55].

These biblical texts help one to understand that the term "antichrist" can be applied to those who are against God's plan of salvation. This would include antipopes who, far from bearing good witness and defending the faith, give in to the temptation of power and paganism. But in no way can it be applied to the pontiffs who guide the Church on the right path and have even given witness to the point of martyrdom. It is regrettable that some groups who are enemies of the Church manipulate biblical texts to present the pope as the antichrist.

55. 2 Thessalonians 2,3

Papal Resignation

Can a pope resign?

Yes, the legislation of the Catholic Church expressed in the Code of Canon Law makes explicit in canon 332: 2 that *"(if) it happens that the Roman Pontiff resigns his office, it is required for validity that the resignation is made freely and properly manifested but not that it is accepted by anyone"*.

What conditions are necessary for papal resignation to be valid?

The Code of Canon Law establishes that in order to be valid, it is required "*that the resignation is made freely and properly manifested*"[56]. It means that it is communicated by the pontiff without coercion and before a qualified audience. Moreover, it must be clear from what moment this renunciation takes effect.

Which popes have resigned throughout history?

Throughout history, at least seven pontiffs have resigned their office, due to various circumstances.

56. Code of Canon Law (1983) Canon 332, 2

The first was St. **Clement** (88-97), third successor of St. Peter. He decided to resign when he was arrested by order of Emperor Nerva and exiled to the Crimea, so as not to leave the Christians of Rome without a guide.

Later, Pope **Pontian** (pontiff from 230 to 235) was condemned "ad metalla", forced labor in the mines of Sardinia, and before leaving the Eternal City he resigned and invited the Christians of Rome to elect a successor. The chosen one was Antero, who died a martyr.

Pope **Silverius** (536-537) was elected pontiff with the support of the Ostrogothic king Theodatus, without knowing that the emperor Justinian I ordered to support the election of another candidate, Vigilius. The latter made his way to Rome with the emperor's letters of support. Silverius was accused of supporting the Goths against the Roman Empire, arrested, stripped of his papal vestments and exiled to Turkey. He was apparently forced to resign. He was replaced by Vigilius (537-555).

Benedict IX (1033-1044) was elected Pope at the age of 25 as a result of pressures from Count Alberic III to the Roman Curia; but expelled because of a popular revolt against his family. His successor, **Sylvester III** (1045) lasted only three months, for he was accused of having usurped the See of Peter, and had to cede it again to Benedict IX (from April to May 1045). It is said that the latter then "sold" the papacy to **Gregory VI**, perhaps to marry; Gregory repented and recognized the purchase, for which he was expelled after 1 year and 7 months of pontificate. Then Clement II (1046-1047) was elected, who died unexpectedly. Benedict IX took advantage of this power vacuum to return to the See of Peter for the third time (1047-1048), until the emperor imposed a new pontiff in 1048 and he retired, accused of simony, i.e., trading in religious offices. Therefore, in the list of popes who have resigned also appears **Gregory VI** (1045-1046), who retired to a monastery.

Honorius II (1124-1130) retired due to illness to a place of prayer, but a successor was not chosen until after his death.

Saint Celestine V (1294) was pope for 5 months and was the protagonist of the historically most famous resignation, as it is mentioned by Dante in his "Divine Comedy". After the death of Nicholas IV on April 4, 1292, the twelve cardinals could not agree on whom to elect as pope. The two opposing factions became entrenched until 27 months after the beginning of the conclave, on July 5, 1294, they elected as pope a hermit, Pietro da Morrone, who took the name of Celestine V. He did not have the strength to face the pressures of the king of Naples, Charles of Anjou, and only four months later decided to resign from the papacy. His successor, Benedict VIII, had him arrested to prevent his rivals from reappointing him pope. He died a few months later, on May 19, 1296, at the age of 87.

Gregory XII (1406-1415). During his pontificate, the Catholic Church was divided between the See of Rome and Avignon. He was elected on the condition that he would resign if the pope elected by the cardinals who paid "obedience" to Avignon also resigned, and that he would not appoint new cardinals if the other pontiff did not. However, he decided to appoint new cardinals. Some cardinals, in agreement with cardinals loyal to Avignon, decided to convene a council in Pisa to depose the two pontiffs and elect a third. Thus, in 1409, they elected Alexander V. As there were three popes, Emperor Sigismund then called a new council to resolve the question, the Council of

Constance, and Gregory XII recognized its validity and resigned the papacy to repair the schism. After his resignation he returned as cardinal and bishop of Frascati. He technically became the first "Roman pontiff emeritus", and is the last pope to be buried outside Rome.

One of the pontiffs of that period was supposedly John XXIII (1410-1417) whose election was not validated by history; therefore, in 1958, Cardinal Angelo Giuseppe Roncalli decided to take the name John XXIII.

Benedict XVI (2005-2013) is the first pontiff to resign in modern times. He communicated his resignation on February 11, 2013, and it took effect on February 28, at 20:00 Rome time. He became "Roman Pontiff Emeritus" and resided in a former monastery in the Vatican Gardens. He died almost ten years later, on December 31, 2022, and is buried in St. Peter's Basilica.

What title does the pope who resigns receive?

After the resignation of Benedict XVI, it was established that he would be called "Pope Emeritus" or "Roman Pontiff Emeritus". In addition, he continued to use the name he assumed when he was elected. Benedict XVI's initial idea was to change his name to "Father Benedict", but he was convinced that it was appropriate for him to keep the title of pontiff. Informally, Pope Francis has said that he considers it more appropriate that if a pope resigns he should become "Bishop of Rome Emeritus".

The idea began to gain momentum after his trip to Mexico, March 23-26, 2012. Benedict had a minor domestic accident in the bathroom, where he sustained a head injury and needed stitches. Jokingly, as he was caring for him, the doctor said, "I don't like you making these trips at all." To which Benedict nodded and said he should stop taking them.

On his return to Rome, the idea that he did not have the strength to respond to the great expectations of Catholics, especially for extraordinary activities such as travel, continued to haunt him. Precisely, he had committed himself to travel to Rio de Janeiro in August 2013 on the occasion of World Youth Day, and he understood that it was an event he could not refuse, but which he would not be able to attend. Added to this were the difficulties in dealing promptly and decisively with the issues that come to the pope's table, as the passing of the years diminished his strength.

He then decided to resign. In April 2012 he mentioned this possibility to Cardinal Tarcisio Bertone. And in August he communicated to him that he had made this decision and that it was final. He let his secretary know in September. In order not to be hasty, he allowed a prudent time to pass before taking the definitive step.

On February 11, 2013, on the occasion of a consistory, he communicated his resignation to the cardinals residing in Rome. He summoned them with the excuse of setting the date for the canonization of Maria Guadalupe Garcia Zavala, from Mexico; and Laura Montoya, from Colombia; and of the Italian martyrs of Otranto, Antonio Primaldo and his 800 companions. At the end of the meeting, at about 11:45 a.m., he explained that he had an "important communication" to make. He then read in Latin his declaration of resignation.

"After having repeatedly examined my conscience before God, I have come to the certainty that my strengths, due to an advanced age, are no longer suited to an adequate exercise of the Petrine ministry. I am well aware that this ministry, due to its essential spiritual nature, must be carried out not only with words and deeds, but no less with prayer and suffering. However, in today's world, subject to so many rapid changes and shaken by questions of deep relevance for the life of faith, in order to govern the barque of Saint Peter and proclaim the Gospel, both strength of mind and body are necessary, strength which in the last few months, has deteriorated in me to the extent that I have had to recognize my incapacity to adequately fulfill the ministry entrusted to me.

For this reason, and well aware of the seriousness of this act, with full freedom I declare that I renounce the ministry of Bishop of Rome, Successor of Saint Peter, entrusted to me by the Cardinals on 19 April 2005, in such a way, that as from 28 February 2013, at 20:00 hours, the See of Rome, the See of Saint Peter, will be vacant and a Conclave to elect the new Supreme Pontiff will have to be convoked by those whose competence it is."

Had there been talk before of a possible resignation of Benedict XVI?

On September 26, 2011, the Vatican spokesman, Federico Lombardi, described as "unfounded" the rumors that Benedict XVI was considering resigning at the age of 85. He was referring to information published by journalist Antonio Socci in the Italian daily

"Libero," according to which the Pontiff was thinking of submitting his resignation in April 2012. "What we know is what the pope has written in his book interview 'Light of the World'. Beyond that I have no other information," the spokesman explained.

In 2010, in the book 'Light of the World', Benedict had said to the German writer Peter Seewald: "If the pope comes to recognize clearly that physically, psychically and mentally he is no longer able to carry out the duties of his office, he has the right and, in certain circumstances, also the duty to resign"[57]. Therefore, even then he had already left open the possibility of resignation, especially in the case of illness that would definitively prevent him from fulfilling his ministry.

What is an antipope?

An "antipope" is someone who proclaims himself or is proclaimed Supreme Pontiff without having been legitimately elected. Therefore, he is not considered the successor of Peter and lacks authority. This title is also given to those who have claimed the title of pope in a non-canonical way, usually in opposition to a specific pontiff or during a period of vacancy of the See.

Therefore, "antipope" does not imply that he defends a doctrine contrary to that taught by the Church, but only the claim, whether usurped or dubious, of the canonical legitimacy of his election and investiture as successor of Peter.

The first antipope dates back to 217, when the legitimate bishop of Rome was Callixtus. His "antipope"

57. Benedict XVI. Light of the World - The Pope, the Church and the Signs of the Times A Conversation with Peter Seewald, Libreria Editrice Vaticana 2010

was Hippolytus, who later died a martyr's death, reconciling himself with the Church. Shortly thereafter, during the pontificate of St. Cornelius (251-253), the antipope Novatian was elected, which led to a schism.

Many antipopes arose in periods of turbulence in the Church, as was the case of the Great Western Schism, related to the transfer of the papal court from Rome to Avignon (France) between the late fourteenth and early fifteenth centuries. On September 20, 1378 the antipope Clement VII was proclaimed against the legitimate pope Urban VI, so that until 1417 there were several popes at the same time.

The last antipope was Felix V, elected on July 24, 1440 against Eugene IV at the Council of Basel. The same council deposed him and he recognized the legitimacy of Nicholas V, who made him a cardinal.

This is the list of antipopes:

Hippolytus (217-235), Novatian (251), Felix II (235-265), Ursinus (366-367), Eulalius (418-419), Lawrence (498; 501-505), Dióscuro (530), Theodore (687), Paschal (687), Constantine II (767-769), Philip (768), John (844), Anastasius (855), Christopher (903-941), Boniface VII (974; 984-985), John XVI (997-998), Gregory (1012), Benedict X (1058-1059), Honorius II (1061-1072), Clement III (1080; 1084-1100), Theodoric (1100), Albert (1102), Sylvester IV (1105-1111), Gregory VIII (1118-1119), Celestine II (1124), Anacletus II (1130-1138), Victor IV (1159-1164), Paschal III (1164-1168), Callistus III (1168-1178), Innocent III (1179-1180), Nicholas V (1328-1330), Clement VII (1378-1394), Benedict XIII (1394-1423), Alexander V (1409-1410), John XXIII (1410-1415), and Felix V (1440-1449).

Since its origins, some authorities of the Church have been persecuted and imprisoned. Peter, the first pope, was imprisoned first in Jerusalem and then in the Mamertine prison in Rome. Other pontiffs were also sent to prison or exile and forced to hard labor.

His third successor, Pope Clement I (88-97), was arrested by order of Emperor Nerva and exiled to Crimea. Later, Pope Pontian (pontiff from 230 to 235) was condemned "ad metalla", that is, to forced labor in the mines of Sardinia.

Pope Formosus (816-896) was also imprisoned in the midst of battles between the Frankish and Germanic phyla.

Centuries later, Napoleon Bonaparte took 81-year-old Pius VI prisoner to France, and he died a few months later.

It is well known the case of Pope Pius VII who left for Paris to officiate on December 2, 1804 the coronation of Napoleon I as emperor, and that in the ceremony he limited himself to anointing him because Napoleon himself decided to crown himself to show that he did not receive the power of the Church. This gesture indicated what was to come years later.

In 1809 Napoleon annexed the Papal States belonging to the Pope and incorporated them into the French Empire. In response, Pius VII excommunicated him. Napoleon then decided to have the pope arrested and taken prisoner to Savona, Grenoble and then to Fontainebleau.

In March 1814, after the emperor's military failures and shortly before he was forced to abdicate, he set the pope free, so that on March 17, 1814 he returned to Rome.

As a gesture of clemency, shortly afterwards, despite the hostility of the Roman population against the French, the Pope gave refuge to Napoleon's mother and her relatives in the Urbe.

Death of the pope

What does the death of a pope mean?

When a pontiff dies, it is not only the end of a man's life, but the end of a stage of the Catholic Church marked by the personality and priorities of that successor of the apostle Peter.

Who is accompanying the pope at the time of his death?

As with all people, he is accompanied by his loved ones, such as his closest collaborators - to whom over the years he has been linked by family ties - or his relatives.

In 2005, when John Paul II was dying, tens of thousands of people came to St. Peter's Square, under the window of his apartment, to show their physical closeness to him. In his room were his main collaborators, including friends who had come from Poland.

In December 2022, when Benedict XVI died, in his room were the people with whom he lived, and the medical staff.

Is it allowed to record the pope's voice or take pictures or video of him during his agony?

In addition to the fact that out of a sense of modesty and humanity no sane person would do so, Vatican law states that "no one is permitted to use any means whatsoever in order to photograph or film the Supreme Pontiff either on his sickbed or after death, or to record his words for subsequent reproduction"[58].

Have photographs ever been taken of the agony of a pope?

Unfortunately, yes. Pius XII's personal physician (1939-1958), the ophthalmologist Riccardo Galeazzi Lisi, photographed the Pope's agony with a small Leica camera and sold the images to the magazine "Paris Match". The publication of the photographs, which showed the Pope lying down receiving oxygen, caused a great scandal and the doctor was expelled from the Italian College of Physicians.

What about the corpse? Is it allowed to take pictures or video of the Pope's corpse?

The Vatican law explains that "if after the Pope's death anyone should wish to take photographs of him for documentary purposes, he must ask permission from the Cardinal Camerlengo of Holy Roman Church, who will not however permit the taking of photographs of the Supreme Pontiff except attired in pontifical vestments"[59].

58. Cfr. Apostolic Constitution Universi Dominici Gregis (February 22, 1996) n. 30
59. Cfr. Apostolic Constitution Universi Dominici Gregis (February 22, 1996) n. 30.

Who breaks the news of the pope's death?

According to the norm, it is officially communicated by the Cardinal Vicar for the City of Rome, who gives the news to the Roman people by means of a special notification[60]. In practice, in fact, it is communicated by the spokesman of the Vatican Press Office through a communiqué. A few minutes later, the bells of St. Peter's Basilica begin to toll with the ringing of the death knell, which resounds throughout the Eternal City.

When John Paul II died on April 2, 2005, first a press release was issued, and minutes later the official announcement was made in St. Peter's Square by the Substitute of the Secretariat of State, Leonardo Sandri, who addressed the thousands of pilgrims who had gathered there to accompany the pope in his agony.

The ceremony of "certification of death and deposition in the coffin", presided over by Cardinal Camerlengo, takes place a few hours later.

Who gives the news to the cardinals, the diplomatic corps and heads of state?

It is up to the Camerlengo to inform the Dean of the College of Cardinals, so that the latter may officially transmit the news to the diplomatic corps and to the heads of state[61].

60. Cfr. Apostolic Constitution Universi Dominici Gregis (22 February 1996) n. 17.
61. Cfr. Apostolic Constitution Universi Dominici Gregis (22 February 1996) n. 17.

What happens when a pope dies?

The first Vatican official to intervene is the pope's physician, in his capacity as director of the Directorate of Health and Hygiene of the Vatican City State. He must prepare "a report after examining the body, in which he notes the death and declares the cause of death; then he does what is necessary for the perfect preservation of the remains, so that they may be exposed with the utmost decorum and respect"[62].

The operative responsible for supervising these operations is the Master of Liturgical Celebrations of the Supreme Pontiff, who begins to prepare the wake.

Once the physician has concluded the examination, the Master of Liturgical Celebrations verifies that "the body of the deceased pontiff is clothed in the white cassock and transferred to the private chapel"[63], where the ritual of "ascertainment of death and deposition in the coffin" will take place.

After his death, the Swiss Guard accompanies and protects the College of Cardinals, which provisionally and with limited executive capacity represents the Holy See until a new successor to the apostle Peter is elected.

What rituals should be performed to verify the death of the pontiff?

The ritual establishes that a first phase or station takes place in a chapel in the house of the deceased Roman Pontiff. It consists of the "ascertainment of the death of the Roman Pontiff in the private chap-

62. Ordo Exsequiarum Romani Pontificis, Second Edition, 2024, n. 21.
63. Ordo Exsequiarum Romani Pontificis, Second Edition, 2024, n. 22.

el of the deceased pontiff, and the deposition of his remains in a wooden and zinc coffin"[64]. It is "a first moment of prayer: all the acts performed express the honor due to the body of the deceased, which with baptism became a Temple of the Holy Spirit, and reaffirm faith in eternal life"[65].

Until November 2024, it was foreseen that the official confirmation of death would take place in "the room of the deceased"[66] and this was followed by a first exposition of his remains in a "suitable place"[67]. That first wake was held with the pope's remains on a catafalque; the coffin was not used until the funeral vigil.

Who should verify the death of the pontiff?

It is verified by his doctors. When a pope dies, "the director of the Directorate of Health and Hygiene of the Vatican City State prepares a report after examining the body, on the finding of death and the cause of death"[68].

The remains are then transferred to the pope's chapel, where this report is read before the Cardinal Camerlengo, accompanied by the Dean of the College of Cardinals, the Master of the Pontifical Liturgical Celebrations and the pope's family members[69]. After hearing the report, the Camerlengo pronounces these words:

"Our pastor, Pope (Name) has died with Christ. We

64. Ordo Exsequiarum Romani Pontificis, Second Edition, 2024, n. 6.
65. Ordo Exsequiarum Romani Pontificis, Second Edition, 2024, n. 7.
66. Ordo Exsequiarum Romani Pontificis, First Edition, 1998, n. 20.
67. Cfr. Ordo Exsequiarum Romani Pontificis, First Edition, 1998, n. 6.
68. Ordo Exsequiarum Romani Pontificis, Second Edition, 2024, n. 21.
69. Cfr. Ordo Exsequiarum Romani Pontificis, Second Edition, 2024, n. 7; and Universi Dominici Gregis, n. 17.

firmly believe that he will live with him. Indeed 'if we have grown into union with him through a death like his, we shall also be united with him in the resurrection' (Rom 6, 5)"[70].

The truth is that the law that regulates the Sede Vacante, the Apostolic Constitution Universi Dominici Gregis, adds that present must also be "the Cleric Prelates of the Apostolic Camera and of the Secretary and Chancellor of the same; the latter shall draw up the official death certificate"[71]. This will not be the case since this organism no longer exists. The 'Apostolic Chamber' was a collegial council formed by ecclesiastics that assisted the Camerlengo in the care of the temporal goods of the Holy See during the Sede Vacante. As of the Pontifical Yearbook 2020 it ceased to appear among the institutions of the Holy See, and with the Apostolic Constitution "Praedicate Evangelium" of March 19, 2022 on the government of the Vatican Curia, it was definitively abolished.

What is the ceremony for the certification of death like?

According to the current edition of the "*Ordo Exsequiarum Romani Pontificis*" ("*Rite of the Funeral Rites of the Roman Pontiff*"), published in November 2024, it is a religious ceremony, "*a moment of prayer*"[72], which takes place in the pope's private chapel, where the remains of the pontiff, already dressed in the white cassock, are transferred[73].

There, the pope's physician will read aloud the report he has prepared containing the medical declaration of death and the causes of death. When he has

70. Ordo Exsequiarum Romani Pontificis, Second Edition, 2024, n. 27.
71. Cfr. Universi Dominici Gregis, n. 17.
72. Ordo Exsequiarum Romani Pontificis, Second Edition, 2024, n. 7..
73. Ordo Exsequiarum Romani Pontificis, Second Edition, 2024, n. 22.

finished, the Camerlengo pronounces these words with which he officially declares the death of the pope:

"Our pastor, Pope (Name) has died with Christ. We firmly believe that he will live with Him".

After a few moments of silence, the Camerlengo invites those present to pray a "Responsory for the Dead", which is the official prayer of the Church for the deceased.

Then, he dresses the corpse in red liturgical vestments, the color of papal mourning, "as in the celebration of the Mass, with the miter and pallium, without the pastoral staff"[74]; and the remains are placed "in a wooden and zinc coffin".

As for the religious symbols that will be present, in addition to the usual ones, "next to the coffin is placed in an appropriate place, the paschal candle"[75], which symbolizes the resurrection of Christ, and the hope of Christians in the resurrection. After lighting the paschal candle, the remains are sprinkled with holy water and a "Salve" is sung to the Virgin Mary.

At the conclusion of this brief religious ceremony, "the Cardinal Camerlengo draws up the authentic death certificate, to which he attaches the certificate of the Director of the Vatican City State Health Services"[76]. This text will be published as soon as possible by the press office of the Holy See.

In the past, it was said that from that time on, the remains of the pope remained "under the vigilance and responsibility of the Master of Liturgical Celebrations." Now the norm merely states that "the Mas-

74. Ordo Exsequiarum Romani Pontificis, Second Edition, 2024, n. 29.
75. Ordo Exsequiarum Romani Pontificis, Second Edition, 2024, n. 29.
76. Cfr. Ordo Exsequiarum Romani Pontificis, Second Edition, 2024, n. 38.

ter of the Pontifical Liturgical Celebrations establishes the hour at which, after everything has been prepared in the private chapel, access will be allowed to those who wish to pray for the deceased pontiff". In any case, it authorizes him to "decide whether the remains should be transported privately to another place, until they are brought to the Vatican Basilica"[77].

The norm also establishes that during this first private wake, "in the place where the remains of the pope will be laid to rest, prayers and ceremonies will be held, in a manner most appropriate to the circumstances". It proposes, for example, "a brief moment of prayer, celebration of the Liturgy of the Hours, celebration of the Word of God, recitation of the rosary"[78].

Is a hammer used to check if the pope is deceased?

In the past, to ascertain the death, Cardinal Camerlengo would give three gentle blows with a hammer on the pontiff's forehead, while calling him by his first name and asking him in Latin "Dormis tu?", "Are you asleep?". He would then pronounce the phrase "Vere Papa mortuus est", "Truly, the Pope is dead". The last time this ritual was performed was in 1878, after the death of Pius IX. John XXIII abolished it definitively. Now it is up to the doctor alone to materially verify the death.

77. Cfr. Ordo Exsequiarum Romani Pontificis, Second Edition, 2024, n. 39.
78. Cfr. Ordo Exsequiarum Romani Pontificis, Second Edition, 2024, n. 40.

What does Cardinal Camerlengo do after finding out that the pope has died?

Once the ceremony of the pontiff's death has concluded, the Camerlengo must seal the pope's work room and other places he used, to prevent intrusions, the falsification of his decisions or the theft of documents.

Also, as soon as possible, he must take possession, in person or through a delegate, of the Vatican Apostolic Palace and the Lateran and Castel Gandolfo Palaces, to exercise their custody and government

He is also in charge of all matters concerning the burial of the pope, unless otherwise provided by the deceased pontiff.

In addition, "he shall deal, in the name of and with the consent of the College of Cardinals, with all matters that circumstances suggest for safeguarding the rights of the Apostolic See and for its proper administration"[79]. In practice, he exercises provisionally the Head of State for matters relating to the Vatican City State and the Holy See.

He cannot act in total autonomy. He will make decisions only in the so-called "particular congregation", "with the help of the three Cardinal Assistants, having sought the views of the College of Cardinals, once only for less important matters, and on each occasion when more serious matters arise". Pope Francis arranged that one of these assisting cardinals be the one who in the Roman Curia is in charge of coordinating the Council for the Economy [80].

79 Cfr. Apostolic Constitution Universi Dominici Gregis (February 22, 1996) n. 17
80. Cfr. Apostolic Constitution "Praedicate Evangelium" (19 March 2022)n. 235 § 3.

What about the staff who regularly live in the Pope's private apartment??

The pope's close collaborators who lived in the same house as him may remain in that accommodation until the day of the burial[81]. From that moment on, no one may occupy any room in the private apartment of the Supreme Pontiff until his successor is elected[82].

When is the papal apartment sealed?

Once the death of the pontiff has been certified, the room and study used by the deceased pope or the one who has resigned must be sealed as soon as possible. However, out of respect for those who were his collaborators, the Camerlengo will wait until after the burial to seal the rest of the rooms in the pontiff's private residence. The idea is that "the personnel who usually live in the private apartment can remain in it until after the burial of the pope, at which time the entire pontifical apartment will be sealed"[83].

What happens if the pope dies outside Rome?

In that case, the College of Cardinals must arrange for a "dignified and reverent transfer of the body to the Basilica of Saint Peter's in the Vatican."[84] This happened, for example, to Paul VI, who died in the summer residence of Castel Gandolfo on August 6, 1978. Pius XII also died there on October 9, 1958.

81. Cfr. Apostolic Constitution Universi Dominici Gregis (February 22, 1996) n. 17.
82. Cfr. Apostolic Constitution Universi Dominici Gregis (February 22, 1996) n. 31.
83. Cfr. Apostolic Constitution Universi Dominici Gregis (February 22, 1996) n. 17.
84. Cfr. Apostolic Constitution Universi Dominici Gregis (February 22, 1996) n. 29.

When is the burial of the pope celebrated?

When established by the plenary meeting of cardinals. The general norm indicates that the burial will take place "between the fourth and sixth day after death"[85].

How have popes died throughout history?

As Carlos Villa Roiz explains in the work "On this rock I will build my Church", among the popes whose cause of death is known, 17 died of old age or natural death, as in the case of John Paul II or Benedict XVI; 65 died of some illness; and 20 died of sudden death. In addition, 31 were martyred and 13 were killed without being considered martyrs. It can be said that three died as a result of an accident.

Who killed those thirteen popes?

These are popes assassinated by rival families who were ambitious to have a pope among their ranks, since the office included the government and management of a large territory. The last pope suspected of being assassinated was Leo X, supposedly poisoned in 1521.

Is it true that John Paul I was assassinated?

No, it is not true. Albino Luciani, born in Forno di Canale (Italy) in 1912, was appointed Patriarch of

85. Cfr. Apostolic Constitution Universi Dominici Gregis (February 22, 1996) n. 13.

Venice in 1969. When he was elected pontiff in August 1978, he united the name of his two predecessors, John XXIII and Paul VI, authors of the Second Vatican Council. His pontificate, marked by his smile, lasted only 33 days, due to a sudden heart attack. At 7:30 a.m. on September 29, 1978, the Vatican Press Office reported that John Paul I had died. The mistake was that the communiqué concealed the truth about who had discovered the body.

"This morning, September 29, 1978, around 5:30, the private secretary of the pope, Rev. P. John Magee, walked into the bedroom of the Holy Father John Paul I because he had not seen him in the chapel -as was the usual custom-, and found him dead in bed with the light on, looking as if he were actually reading. The physician was called immediately, and he confirmed the pope's death, which supposedly happened around 11 pm of the previous day, the cause having been "sudden death due to an acute myocardial infarction".

In reality, the body was discovered by two of the four nuns who were in charge of his domestic service, but at the time the Vatican considered it inelegant to explain that two women had entered the pope's bedroom. One of them, Sister Margherita Marin, of the Congregation of Maria Bambina, recounted those hours:

"As I did every day, my task was to prepare the chapel first thing in the morning for him to celebrate Mass. In the meantime, Sister Vincenza would prepare coffee for the pope and leave it at his bedroom door for him to drink as soon as he woke up.

I remember, however, that we were in the chapel, and we were worried because we had been waiting for a long time and the pope was not coming. So I said to Sister, 'See what's going on....' When we approached his room, we saw that the coffee cup was still on the bedroom door. Sister Vincenza knocked on the door and when there was no answer, she opened it. The light was on, and the pope was sitting motionless on the bed, with his glasses on and his hands on his chest, as if he had fallen asleep reading. He had some papers in his hand. We called the secretaries, Cardinal Jean-Marie Villot came[86]*. Two other priests whom I did not know came. I heard them say that they did not know how to announce it.... One repeated, 'What do we say to the world now that he had conquered it with his smile?' It was very painful for us. But the doctor told us that the pope had not suffered. He had a sudden heart attack. He left us too quickly and too soon..."*[87]

His niece, Lina Petri, was also categorical:

"In our family we have never believed in plots, we have never had any suspicions. I think it is an insult to intelligence to insinuate that my uncle John Paul I was assassinated"[88].

Which popes have died because of accidents?

There are three. In 1144, Lucius II died when a stone fell on him while he was reviewing his troops. Another is John XXI (1276-1277), who died when part of the roof of the library he was working on in the Papal Palace in Viterbo collapsed. In 1823, Pius VII tripped and broke his hip. The injury led to serious complications that later led to his death.

86. Cardinal Jean-Marie Villot (1905-1979) was appointed Secretary of State of the Holy See by Paul VI in 1969. He remained in that position until his death in 1979; therefore, he continued to exercise it during the pontificate of John Paul I and the first months of the pontificate of John Paul II.
87. Personal interview with the author.
88. Personal interview with the author.

What have been the shortest pontificates in history?

Popes Sisinus (8th century) and Damasus II (11th century) ruled the Catholic Church for only 20 days.

In 1241, Celestine IV died 17 days after his election, without being crowned. His death is attributed to the harsh conditions of the conclave. Of the twelve cardinals who participated, two died during the confinement. The other cardinals fled Rome after his death, fearing that a new conclave would be called. Indeed, it took another two years before a new conclave was convened.

Pius III, whose civil name was Francesco Nanni Todeschini Piccolomini (1439-1503), was cardinal secretary of state to five popes and was elected in 1503 to the papal chair, but died 10 days after his coronation from an attack of gout.

Urban VII (1521-1590) died 12 days after his election, a victim of malaria. His pontificate was the shortest in history.

Leo XI (1535-1605) contracted a cold while taking possession of the Basilica of St. John Lateran and died 17 days after his coronation.

In 1978, John Paul I ruled the Church for only 33 days.

Wake and funeral of the Pope

What documents indicate what the wake and burial of the pontiff should be like?

The main one is the "*Ordo Exsequiarum Romani Pontificis*", or "*Rite of the Funeral Rites of the Roman Pontiff*", which contains all the provisions for the funeral rites of the popes. The current edition bears the date June 29, 2024, but was released in November of that year.

The text is based on the document "*De funere Summi Pontificis*" of 1978, which was implemented that year for the funerals of Paul VI and John Paul I. In 1998, John Paul II updated it and entitled it "*Ordo Exsequiarum Romani Pontificis*". It was used for his funeral and, with some adaptations, for that of Benedict XVI. In 2024, Pope Francis modified some elements and published a second edition. Curiously, it does not specify a specific ritual for the death of an emeritus pope.

What are the Pope's funeral services?

The funeral rite of the Roman Pontiff is divided into three stations or phases. The first takes place in the private chapel of the deceased pontiff, the second in the Vatican Basilica and the third at the burial place[89].

What should the Pope's wake be like?

After the ceremony of the confirmation of death, the Master of Liturgical Ceremonies of the Supreme Pontiff dresses the pope in his white cassock with "the liturgical vestments of red, as in the celebration of the Mass, with the mitre and pallium, without the papal pastoral staff", and his remains are placed in a wooden and zinc coffin[90]. Red is the color of papal mourning. He will also wear the white skullcap. He will have the pectoral cross around his neck and will wear an episcopal ring symbolizing his fidelity to the Church[91].

The Apostolic Constitution "Universi Dominici Gregis" establishes that in one of the first "general congregations", the cardinals should "fix the day, hour and manner in which the body of the deceased Pope shall be brought to the Vatican Basilica in order to be exposed for the homage of the faithful"[92]. Until then it will remain in his private chapel or in "another place" established by the Master of Liturgical Celebrations of the Supreme Pontiff, "where access will be allowed to those who wish to pray for the deceased pontiff"[93].

Until 2024, the wake was scheduled to be held with the remains of the pontiff on a catafalque. Now, they will be inside a coffin.

89. Cfr. Ordo Exsequiarum Romani Pontificis, Second Edition, 2024, n. 5.
90. Cfr. Ordo Exsequiarum Romani Pontificis, Second Edition, 2024, n. 29.
91. Cfr. "Sede Apostolica Vacante. Storia - Legislazione - Riti - Luoghi e cose". Ufficio delle Celebrazioni Liturgiche del Sommo Pontefice. Vatican City, 2005. P. 76. "Esposizione della salma".
92. Cfr. Apostolic Constitution Universi Dominici Gregis (February 22, 1996) n. 13, a).
93. Ordo Exsequiarum Romani Pontificis, Second Edition, 2024, n. 39.

Why is the color of papal mourning red?

There are usually two reasons for this: first, to imitate the liturgical custom of Orthodox Church during days of mourning; and second, to remember that many popes have died as martyrs[94].On the other hand, in the past red was linked to the dignity of monarchs and emperors. In any case, red has not always been used by popes as a symbol of mourning. Some in the past were buried dressed in black or violet.

Is the Pope's corpse embalmed?

Currently, the "Ordo Exsequiarum Romani Pontificis", the document that guides the ceremonies after the death of the Pope, states only that the director of the Vatican City State Sanitary Services "does what is necessary for the perfect preservation of the remains, so that they are exposed with the utmost decorum and respect"[95], but does not mention that it is necessary to embalm or treat the corpse.

In the past, it was customary to embalm the bodies of popes, unless they themselves had ordered otherwise, as did Pius X (1903-1914). At least since the death of John Paul II, the corpse is not embalmed but "treated" to slow its decomposition during the days of the wake.

From Sixtus V to Leo XIII, that is, from 1590 to 1903, the entrails of the embalmed popes were taken to the crypt of the church of Saints Vincent and Anastasius, on the left side of the square of the Trevi Fountain in Rome.

94. Cfr. "Dizionario di erudizione storico-ecclesiastica da San Pietro sino ai nostri giorni. Volume 6 - 'Cadavere'", Gaetano Moroni (1802-1883).
95. Ordo Exsequiarum Romani Pontificis, Second Edition, 2024, n. 21.

Are there any rules about the pope's coffin?

The Vatican establishes that the pope must be buried "in a wooden and zinc coffin," which is the usual coffin used when the body is to be buried and not cremated. On the top of the zinc cover will be engraved "a cross, the coat of arms of the deceased pontiff and a plaque with the pope's name and the duration of his life and Petrine ministry." The exterior of the coffin, made of wood, will also have a cross and the coat of arms of the pope[96].

Until 2024, the norm was to use a triple casket. The first was usually made of cypress, lined with crimson velvet and covered with a zinc coffin, sealed by welding. The third coffin, the one in plain view, was made of oak. Also, in the past, the last time was in 1978 when John Paul I died, lead was used instead of zinc, which made the coffin extremely heavy and difficult to transport.

What rituals are performed before closing the coffin?

Tradition dictates that the pontiff be buried in a red chasuble, the color of papal mourning, and laid in a coffin made of wood and zinc. After several days of vigil in St. Peter's Basilica, the pope's coffin is closed during a private ceremony, preferably held on the eve of the funeral[97].

Before closing it, a series of gestures must be fulfilled, during a ritual in the presence of the Cardinal Camerlengo, the three cardinals who head the episcopal, presbyteral and diaconal orders, the archpriest

96. Ordo Exsequiarum Romani Pontificis, Second Edition, 2024, n. 76; and "Sede Apostolica Vacante. Storia – Legislazione – Riti – Luoghi e cose". Ufficio delle Celebrazioni Liturgiche del Sommo Pontefice. Vatican City, 2005.
97. Ordo Exsequiarum Romani Pontificis, Second Edition, 2024, n. 12.

of the basilica where he is to be buried, the cardinal who served as Secretary of State, the Pope's Vicar for the Diocese of Rome, the substitute for the Secretary of State, the Prefect of the Pontifical Household, the Pope's Almsgiver, the Vice Camerlengo, a representation of canons of the basilica and of the penitentiaries, the Pope's secretary and the relatives of the deceased. The Master of Papal Liturgical Celebrations "may also grant permission to other persons to be present at this act"[98].

The Master of Papal Liturgical Celebrations will have drawn up an official record "recalling the life and most important works of the deceased, for which we will give thanks to God"[99]. During the ceremony, he will read the text aloud, and some of those present will sign two copies of the document. One of them will be placed in a "metal" tube - in the past the metal was lead - with the seal of the Office of Liturgical Ceremonies of the Pontiff, and the other will be kept in the archives of this department[100].

The face of the deceased pope is also covered with a white silk veil, "in the lively hope that he may contemplate the face of God the Father, together with the Blessed Virgin Mary and the Saints"[101]. In the past, the veil was spread by the pope's secretary and the Master of Papal Liturgical Celebrations, but now it is foreseen that only the Master of Papal Liturgical Celebrations will spread the veil[102]. Afterwards, the Camerlengo sprinkles the corpse with holy water.

The Master of Papal Liturgical Celebrations also places inside the coffin a cloth bag with coins minted during the pontificate, which according to custom

98. Cfr. Ordo Exsequiarum Romani Pontificis, Second Edition, 2024, n. 66.
99. Cfr. Ordo Exsequiarum Romani Pontificis, Second Edition, 2024, n. 70.
100. Cfr. Ordo Exsequiarum Romani Pontificis, Second Edition, 2024, nn. 71 and 75.
101. Cfr. Ordo Exsequiarum Romani Pontificis, Second Edition, 2024, n. 70.
102. Cfr. Ordo Exsequiarum Romani Pontificis, Second Edition, 2024, n. 74.

indicate how long the pontificate has lasted: a gold one is placed for each year, a silver one for each extra month since the anniversary of his election; and more bronze ones, for the days. For example, to remember the 7 years, 10 months and 9 days that Benedict's pontificate lasted, seven gold, ten silver and nine bronze medals were introduced.

Where is the first wake held?

It depends on what the pope has established in his will, although there are some general rules in case he does not leave anything in his will. During the ceremony of confirmation of death, the Master of Liturgical Ceremonies of the Supreme Pontiff dresses the Pope with "the liturgical vestments of red, as in the celebration of the Mass, with the mitre and pallium, without the papal pastoral", and his remains are placed in a wooden and zinc coffin[103]. Afterwards, and until begins the public wake in the Vatican Basilica, the remains will remain in the private chapel of the deceased pope, or in "another place" established by the Master of Liturgical Celebrations of the Supreme Pontiff, "where access will be allowed to those who wish to pray for the deceased pontiff"[104].

Therefore, the Master of Papal Liturgical Celebrations decides when the lying-in-state will be opened in which the pope's body will be veiled until the cardinals decide the date on which it will be taken to St. Peter's Basilica; and whether this will take place in his private chapel or elsewhere.

In the past, in that first phase, it was "customary for the remains of the Roman Pontiff to be watched over

103. Cfr. Ordo Exsequiarum Romani Pontificis, Second Edition, 2024, n. 29.
104. Cfr. Ordo Exsequiarum Romani Pontificis, Second Edition, 2024, n. 39.

by the penitentiaries of the Vatican Basilica who wear a red stole and alternate at least two at a time by the coffin, praying for the deceased[105].

In 2005, the remains of John Paul II were first taken to the Clementine Hall of the Apostolic Palace, where he received the homage of the Vatican Curia and the Diplomatic Corps, before being transferred to the basilica. Likewise, on January 1, 2023, Benedict XVI's wake was opened at his own residence, the Mater Ecclesiae monastery in the Vatican Gardens.

This first wake is brief, because once the cardinals have arranged it, the second phase of the funeral begins, and the remains of the pope are solemnly transferred to St. Peter's Basilica so that pilgrims who wish to attend can do so, until the funeral begins. Paul VI and John Paul I were taken there for the public wake the day after their deaths; John Paul II and Benedict XVI, two days later.

What should the pope's mortuary chapel look like?

It is prepared by the Master of the Liturgical Celebrations of the Supreme Pontiff, assisted by the Masters of Ceremonies and other collaborators. In addition to what has been established by the Pope, "next to the body of the Supreme Pontiff is placed, in a suitable place, the paschal candle"[106] which will be lit and represents hope in the resurrection.

The idea is that there "prayers and ceremonies should be offered in the manner most suitable to the circumstances". He proposes, for example, "a brief moment of prayer, celebration of the Liturgy of the

105. Cfr. Ordo Exsequiarum Romani Pontificis, First Edition, 1998, n. 40.
106. Cfr. Ordo Exsequiarum Romani Pontificis, Second Edition, 2024, n. 29.

Hours, celebration of the Word of God, recitation of the rosary"[107].

When are the remains of the Pope transferred to St. Peter's Basilica for the public wake?

When the plenary meeting of the cardinals decides. It is one of the first decisions they will make. In general, it is usually made about 24-48 hours after his death. Paul VI and John Paul I were brought there for the public wake the day after their deaths; John Paul II and Benedict XVI, two days later. The second phase of the papal funeral begins there.

What does the second part of the funeral consist of?

It consists of the transfer of the remains of the deceased pope to the Vatican Basilica for the public wake.

How are the remains of the pope transferred to St. Peter's Basilica?

The remains are carried in procession, accompanied by all the cardinals present in Rome. When they cross the threshold of the basilica, the so-called "Litany of the Saints" begins to be intoned, answered with the phrase "Pray for him"[108].

The remains stay in the Vatican Basilica, since there "he often exercised his ministry as Bishop of

107. Cfr. Ordo Exsequiarum Romani Pontificis, Second Edition, 2024, n. 40.
108. Cfr. Ordo Exsequiarum Romani Pontificis, Second Edition, 2024, n. 57.

the Church in Rome and Pastor of the universal Church"[109]. They will remain on display for several days so that pilgrims can say goodbye to him.

Until 1958, when Pius XII died, they were held in the Chapel of the Blessed Sacrament. Currently, this wake must be held in the central nave of St. Peter's Basilica, near the tomb of the first apostle. The rule explicitly states that "the coffin is placed before the altar of Confession, facing the people"[110].

When is the funeral mass for the pope celebrated?

The solemn funeral is celebrated on the date established by the plenary meeting of cardinals. The general norm indicates that the burial will take place between the fourth and sixth day after death "except for special reasons"[111].

Where does the solemn public funeral take place?

It should be celebrated "in the square of the papal basilica of St. Peter". In the past, funerals were held inside the basilica, in the Chapel of the Canons. The funerals of Pius XI (1939), Pius XII (1958) and John XXIII (1963) were held in the apse, where the catafalque was also installed. The funerals of Paul VI (1978) and John Paul I (1978) were celebrated with an open-air Mass in St. Peter's Square. The same was done for the funerals of John Paul II (2005) and Benedict XVI (died in 2022).

109. Cfr. Ordo Exsequiarum Romani Pontificis, Second Edition, 2024, n. 46.
110. Cfr. Ordo Exsequiarum Romani Pontificis, Second Edition, 2024, n. 58.
111. Cfr. Apostolic Constitution Universi Dominici Gregis (February 22, 1996) n. 13.

Who is invited to the pope's funeral?

The ceremony is open to all who wish to attend. Seats of honor are usually reserved for official delegations sent by governments.

Are there any rules for members of the diplomatic corps attending the funeral?

They must dress in full dress, without decorations, as a sign of mourning.

How do the pope's funerals differ from those of other Christians?

Apart from the solemnity of the ceremony and the place where it is celebrated, the prayers of the ritual have very few differences with respect to the funerals of other bishops, although there are some specific ones to underline the specificity of the office of the Bishop of Rome.

Another specific difference is the ritual of "last commendation and farewell" which takes place after the final blessing and consists of three parts: first, a "supplication of the Church of Rome presided over by the Cardinal Vicar" next to the coffin; next, a prayer "of the Eastern Churches" led by an Eastern Patriarch; and third, a prayer by the Cardinal Dean on behalf of the whole Church.

How does the Mass conclude?

After the Mass, the cardinals who celebrated the Mass leave in procession, followed by the coffin carried by the "sediari". As the coffin enters the Vatican Basilica, the Magnificat[112] is sung. Some of them will participate in the third and final part of the funeral rite.

What is the third phase of the pope's funeral?

The third and final phase of the pope's funeral is the rite of burial or entombment.

112. Cfr. Ordo Exsequiarum Romani Pontificis, Second Edition, 2024, n. 109.

The burial

When is the pope buried?

After the funeral mass, burial takes place immediately[113].

Where is the pope's burial?

If the burial is in St. Peter's Basilica, after the funeral mass the remains are transferred to the Vatican Grottoes (the crypt beneath the basilica where the tombs of many of St. Peter's successors are preserved) through the so-called Door of Prayer[114].

If the pope is buried elsewhere, "the Master of Pontifical Liturgical Ceremonies establishes how this is to be done and indicates the persons accompanying him"[115].

What does the burial rite consist of?

The rite of burial takes place in the crypt where the coffin will be buried. It is presided over by the Cardi-

113. Cfr. Ordo Exsequiarum Romani Pontificis, Second Edition, 2024, n. 16.
114. Cfr. Ordo Exsequiarum Romani Pontificis, Second Edition, 2024, n. 110.
115. Ibid.

nal Camerlengo. During this rite, the coffin is sealed and placed in the sepulcher[116].

Who can participate in the burial rite?

In addition to the Cardinal Camerlengo, the cardinals who preside over the three orders of the hierarchy of cardinals, the archpriest of the basilica where the pontiff is buried, the Cardinal Secretary of State, the Cardinal Vicar of Rome, the substitute of the Secretary of State, the Prefect of the Papal Household, the Pope's almoner, the Vice-Camerlengo, the Master of Papal Liturgical Celebrations, a representation of the canons of the basilica, the relatives of the deceased and other persons indicated by the Master of Papal Liturgical Celebrations[117].

How is the Pope's coffin sealed?

The seals of the Cardinal Camerlengo, of the Prefecture of the Papal Household, of the Office of Liturgical Ceremonies of the Supreme Pontiff, and if he is buried in the Vatican Grottoes, also that of the Vatican Chapter[118] are impressed on the coffin. The coffin is then placed in the tomb and for the last time the Camerlengo sprinkles it with holy water. In the meantime, a hymn to the Virgin Mary, for example the "Salve Regina", is recited.

Then a notary - if the burial is in St. Peter's, the notary of the Vatican Chapter; otherwise, the corresponding notary - draws up the act that attests that

116. Cfr. Ordo Exsequiarum Romani Pontificis, Second Edition, 2024, n. 17.
117. Cfr. Ordo Exsequiarum Romani Pontificis, Second Edition, 2024, n. 110.
118. Cfr. Ordo Exsequiarum Romani Pontificis, Second Edition, 2024, n. 120.
119. Cfr. Ordo Exsequiarum Romani Pontificis, Second Edition, 2024, n. 123.

the burial has taken place in that precise place, and reads it to those present. It is signed by the Cardinal Camerlengo, the Prefect of the Papal Household, the Master of Papal Liturgical Celebrations and the Notary[119].

Until the funeral of Benedict XVI, this ceremony was much longer because a triple coffin was used. According to the norm in force until then, the first one, made of cypress wood, was "tied with red ribbons on which are placed the seals of the Apostolic Chamber, of the Prefecture of the Papal Household, of the Office of the Liturgical Ceremonies of the Supreme Pontiff and of the Vatican Chapter" or of the Chapter or council of canons of the basilica where the pope is buried[120].

Then, it was covered with zinc plates and on top of these, other wooden ones, "and immediately it is salted and on the metal the seals of the same offices are printed"[121]. In addition, although the notary drew up the act of burial and read it before those present, it was established that "in a second moment", "a delegate of the Cardinal Camerlengo and a delegate of the Prefect of the Pontifical Household would separately draw up the documents attesting that the burial had taken place; the first in the presence of the members of the Apostolic Chamber and the other before the Prefect of the Pontifical Household"[122]. This is no longer considered necessary.

119. Cfr. Ordo Exsequiarum Romani Pontificis, Second Edition, 2024, n. 123.
120. Cfr. Ordo Exsequiarum Romani Pontificis, First Edition, 1998, n. 130.
121. Ibid.
122. Cfr. Ordo Exsequiarum Romani Pontificis, First Edition, 1998, n. 132, and Apostolic Constitution Universi Dominici Gregis (February 22, 1996) n. 28.

Each pontiff can decide where he wishes to be buried, although if he does not give any indication it is understood that his remains will be taken to St. Peter's Basilica. In fact, most of the pontiffs rest in the crypt beneath St. Peter's Basilica, in the Vatican Grottoes. Many others requested to be buried in other basilicas in Rome or in churches in Italy, France and even Spain.

In the catacombs of St. Callixtus in Rome there is a chapel with several tombs of pontiffs. Also in Rome there are common cemeteries that keep their remains.

In the Vatican are buried 149 of the 266 pontiffs that have been, because until the beginning of the last century many requested that their remains be taken to a church linked to their own history in Rome or even outside the Eternal City.

Except for Leo XIII, all the popes of the 20th and 21st centuries are buried in the "Vatican grottoes", in the crypt near the tomb of St. Peter. The last one was Benedict XVI, buried on January 5, 2023 in the same tomb previously occupied by John XXIII and John Paul II. While the remains of the latter were transferred from the Vatican grottoes to the basilica when they were beatified, those of Paul VI and John Paul I remain in the crypt.

Francis said in 2023 that he wishes to be buried in the Basilica of Santa Maria Maggiore in Rome[123]. The last pontiff not to be buried in the Vatican was Leo XIII, who was born near Rome in 1810 and died in 1903. Being a Roman, his remains were moved to the

123. Cfr. "The Successor. My memories of Benedict XVI". Pope Francis and Javier Martínez-Brocal. Barcelona, Editorial Planeta (2024)

Basilica of St. John Lateran in 1924 to recall his link with the cathedral of the Eternal City.

Also Pius IX (1792-1878) requested in his will that he be buried in the Basilica of San Lorenzo Outside the Walls in Rome, where he was transferred in 1881. The funeral procession was attacked on a bridge over the Tiber by a group of anti-clerical Romans, who threatened to throw the coffin into the river. They reproached him for having delayed the unity of Italy.

Is it true that the pope is buried in a triple coffin?

This is no longer the case. Francis established in 2024 that popes be buried in a coffin "made of wood and zinc". Zinc is used in the coffins of those who wish to be buried and not cremated.

Until then, the norm established that the pontiff was buried in a triple coffin. The remains of the pontiff were placed for the funeral in a first wooden coffin[124]. Before burial, the coffin was tied with a red ribbon sealed with sealing wax from the Apostolic Chamber, the Papal Household, the Canons of the basilica where he was buried and the Office of Liturgical Ceremonies. This coffin was then placed in a larger zinc coffin, 4 millimeters thick. And this one, once sealed, was covered with another one made of oak wood.

Are there any documents on the burial of the pope?

Yes. "If the burial takes place in the papal basilica of St. Peter, the notary of the Vatican Chapter - or

124. Cfr. Ordo Exsequiarum Romani Pontificis, First Edition, 1998, n. 12.

another notary if the burial takes place elsewhere - draws up the authentic act declaring the performance of the burial and reads it to those present. The document is then signed by the Camerlengo of the Holy Roman Church, the prefect of the Papal Household, the Master of Liturgical Ceremonies and the notary".

Do popes make wills?

This is a personal decision, left to his free will, although it is usual for him to leave a written will. The law establishes that "if the deceased Supreme Pontiff has made a will concerning his belongings, bequeathing letters and private documents, and has named an executor thereof, it is the responsibility of the latter to determine and execute, in accordance with the mandate received from the testator, matters concerning the private property and writings of the deceased Pope. The executor will give an account of his activities only to the new Supreme Pontiff".

Paul VI (1963-1978) died on August 6 and the cardinals read his testament on the 10th, before making it public. The pope had written this text on June 30, 1965, and completed it with two additions in 1972 and 1973.

John Paul II's will was published on April 7, 2005, five days after his death. It was a spiritual text with some indications about his funeral. He began writing it in 1979 and finished it in 2000. He used to reread it every year during his spiritual exercises.

The testament of Benedict XVI (2005-2013) was published a few hours after his death, on December 31, 2022. In his case it was a rich text of a strictly spiritual nature written in 2006.

What are "novendiali"?

These are the nine Masses for the dead that are celebrated for the pontiff during nine consecutive days, beginning with the funeral Mass. Once the congregation of cardinals decides on the date of the funeral, a special Mass for the dead - or "novendiali" - is celebrated in St. Peter's Basilica for the following eight days[125].

They are ceremonies open to all, but each day specific participation is entrusted to a different group to manifest their special bond with the pope. "This variety of assemblies shows the scope of the ministry of the Supreme Pastor and the universality of the Church of Rome"[126]. They are[127]:

Day I: Papal Chapel (for the pontiff's funeral).

Day II: The dependents and faithful of Vatican City

Day III: The Church of Rome

Day IV: The Chapters of the Patriarchal Basilicas

Day V: The Papal Chapel

Day VI: The Roman Curia

Day VII: The Eastern Churches

Day VIII: Members of Institutes of Consecrated Life

Day IX: The Papal Chapel

125. Cfr. Ordo Exsequiarum Romani Pontificis, Second Edition, 2024, n. 124.
126. Cfr. Ordo Exsequiarum Romani Pontificis, Second Edition, 2024, n. 125.
127. Ibid.

Historically, in non-religious circles, “novendiali” marked a time of mourning in memory of a deceased person, which concluded on the ninth day with a special dinner.

Vacancy of the Holy See

When does the "Sede Vacante" or vacancy period of the Apostolic See officially begin?

The episcopal see that goes back to the apostle Peter becomes vacant when the one who occupies it, the pope, resigns or dies. From that moment begins the period of "Sede Vacante" characterized by a series of protocols and mechanisms intended to ensure the legitimacy of the election of the successor.

Who is in charge in the Church when a pope dies or resigns?

According to the apostolic constitution "Universi Dominici Gregis", when a pontiff resigns or dies, the period of "Sede Vacante" begins, and "the government of the Church is entrusted to the College of Cardinals solely for the dispatch of ordinary business and of matters which cannot be postponed, and for the preparation of everything necessary for the election of the new Pope"[128].

Therefore, the College of Cardinals will only be able to make generic decisions or decisions that re-

128. Cfr. Apostolic Constitution Universi Dominici Gregis (February 22, 1996) n. 2.

quire an immediate response.

Likewise, during the same period, the provisional head of state of the Vatican City State - the "temporal" interests of the Holy See - remains in the hands of Cardinal Camerlengo.

Is there any ecclesiastical authority that can claim the power or jurisdiction of the pope when he dies or resigns?

While the Apostolic See is vacant, no one, not even the College of Cardinals or the Cardinal Camerlengo, has any power or jurisdiction over matters pertaining to the Supreme Pontiff. Therefore, preventively, John Paul II declared "null and void any act of power or jurisdiction pertaining to the Roman Pontiff during his lifetime or in the exercise of his office" that is put in place during the Sede Vacante, even if decided by the full College of Cardinals.[129].

Can the cardinals make any decision during the Sede Vacante regarding, for example, a dogma, a canonization or the appointment of a bishop?

No, they cannot. "The College of Cardinals has no power or jurisdiction in matters which pertain to the Supreme Pontiff during his lifetime or in the exercise of his office; such matters are to be reserved completely and exclusively to the future Pope"[130]. So much so that in the event that they did so, John Paul II in advance declared "null and void any act of power or jurisdiction pertaining to the Roman Pontiff dur-

129. Cfr. Apostolic Constitution Universi Dominici Gregis (February 22, 1996) n. 1.
130. Cfr. Apostolic Constitution Universi Dominici Gregis (February 22, 1996) n. 1.

ing his lifetime or in the exercise of his office which the College of Cardinals might see fit to exercise, beyond the limits expressly permitted in the apostolic constitution 'Universi Dominici Gregis'"[131].

What offices cease with the death or resignation of a Pope?

When the Pope dies, all the high offices of the Vatican Curia, including the Cardinal Secretary of State, automatically cease, since "all heads of curial institutions and members cease from their office"[132]. The norm mentions a few exceptions.

"Those exempt from this rule are the Major Penitentiary, who continues to carry out the ordinary business within his competence and refers all matters to the College of Cardinals which otherwise would have been referred to the Roman Pontiff, and the Almoner of His Holiness, who continues to exercise the works of charity, according to the same criteria followed during the Pontificate and remains at the service of the College of Cardinals until the election of the new Roman Pontiff"[133].

Nor does the Vatican's number three, the replacement for the Secretariat of State, cease.

On the other hand, the Cardinal Camerlengo immediately takes office.

A special role will be played by the Cardinal Coordinator of the Council for the Economy, who will be responsible for assisting the Cardinal Camerlengo in

131. Ibid.
132. Cfr. Apostolic Constitution "Praedicate Evangelium", March 19, 2022. n. 18.
133. Ibid.

the management of ordinary matters[134].

Since the heads of all the Dicasteries are dismissed, "when the See is vacant, the Secretaries [of these departments] attend to the ordinary governance of curial institutions, taking care of ordinary business only. They must be confirmed in office by the Roman Pontiff within three months of his election"[135]. The secretary of each dicastery is, in general, the number two in that department. Within three months of the election of the Roman pontiff, the new pope must confirm or replace them in office.

Another important person for certain practical decisions is the secretary of the College of Cardinals, a position that coincides with that of secretary of the Dicastery for Bishops.

Also during this period, the Master of the Pontifical Liturgical Celebrations, during the funeral rites and the conclave, should exercise certain special functions and make specific decisions[136].

With the death of the pope there are no changes for apostolic nuncios, bishops, parish priests, chaplains, superiors of religious communities, rectors of seminaries and other positions that depend on the bishops in their own territories, and who continue normally to exercise their mission. For this reason, neither the Cardinal Vicar of the Diocese of Rome nor the Cardinal Archpriest of the Vatican Basilica, who is Vicar General for Vatican City, cease from their office[137].

134. Cfr. Apostolic Constitution "Praedicate Evangelium" (19 March 2022) n. 235 § 3. 235 § 3.
135. Cfr. Apostolic Constitution "Praedicate Evangelium", March 19, 2022. N. 18.
136. Ibid.
137. Cfr. Apostolic Constitution Universi Dominici Gregis (February 22, 1996) N. 14.

Summarizing, what are the relevant positions during the Sede Vacante period?

They are the Cardinal Dean, the Cardinal Camerlengo, the Cardinal Coordinator of the Council for the Economy, the Master of Papal Liturgical Celebrations, the Secretary of the College of Cardinals and the Substitute of the Secretary of State.

What are the 'ordinary' and what are the 'extraordinary' issues on which they can and cannot make decisions?

In terms of the governance of the Holy See, ordinary matters are those that would not require an audience with the pope to be resolved[138].

Who are the most important cardinals during the period of Sede Vacante?

During the Sede Vacante there are two cardinals who exercise special functions and have a greater public presence: the "Cardinal Dean" and the "Cardinal Camerlengo".

Also relevant are the three "cardinal assistants". One of them is the cardinal coordinator of the Council for the Economy[139]; and the other two are elected for three-day shifts, to assist the cardinal Camerlengo or, in his absence, the dean of the College of Cardinals until a new Camerlengo is elected.

138. Cfr. This was clarified in the General Regulations of the Roman Curia of 1992 (art. 44 § 1). In its successive versions (1999 and 2011), it refers directly to the provisions of the Universi Dominici Gregis.
139. Cfr. Constitución Apostólica "Praedicate Evangelium" (19 de marzo de 2022) n. 235 § 3.

What does the "Cardinal Dean" do during the Sede Vacante?

The "Cardinal Dean" immediately notifies the diplomatic corps and heads of state of the pope's death or resignation. In addition, he requests all cardinals to present themselves in Rome to elect a new pontiff together. He is in charge of presiding over the cardinals' meetings prior to the conclave.

As those residing outside of Rome arrive, the Cardinal Dean will take an oath from the Cardinal electors that they will comply with and enforce the Apostolic Constitution "Universi Dominici Gregis", which regulates pontifical succession.

If he is under 80 years of age, he also presides over the conclave and when a candidate has obtained more than two-thirds of the votes, he must ask him if he accepts the election and how he wishes to be called; and if the new pope is not a bishop, he himself will ordain him immediately before his name is publicly announced.

If he is over 80 years of age and cannot enter the conclave, he will be replaced in the Sistine Chapel by the Cardinal Vice-Dean; if he is also over that age, by the oldest Cardinal Elector, according to the order of precedence[140].

Likewise, if there is no cardinal Camerlengo, the cardinal dean exercises his functions until one has been elected.

140. Cfr. Apostolic Constitution Universi Dominici Gregis (February 22, 1996) N. 9.

What does the "Cardinal Camerlengo" do during the Sede Vacante?

The functions of the Cardinal Camerlengo come into effect only during the period of Sede Vacante. After the resignation or death of a pope, he is responsible for the custody and administration of all the goods and temporal rights of the Holy See until a new pontiff is elected. Vatican law entrusts him to "deal, in the name of and with the consent of the College of Cardinals, with all matters that circumstances suggest for safeguarding the rights of the Apostolic See and for its proper administration"[141].

In practice, he represents the head of state of the Vatican City State during the Sede Vacante, on behalf of the College of Cardinals, although he has the power to make decisions only on ordinary matters. To do so, he is assisted by three cardinal electors present in Rome; one of them must be the cardinal coordinator of the Council for the Economy[142], and the other two will be chosen by lot and renewed every three days. With them he holds periodic meetings, one or more each day, called "particular congregations". The measures they take can only be revoked by a majority vote of the "General Congregation" or plenary of cardinals.

On the other hand, it falls to the Cardinal Camerlengo to "officially ascertain the Pope's death", "place seals on the Pope's study and bedroom, making provision that the personnel who ordinarily reside in the private apartment can remain there until after the burial of the Pope, at which time the entire papal apartment will be sealed; he must notify the Cardinal Vicar for Rome of the Pope's death, whereupon the

141. Cfr. Apostolic Constitution Universi Dominici Gregis (February 22, 1996) n. 17.
142. Cfr. Apostolic Constitution "Praedicate Evangelium" (19 March 2022) n. 235 § 3.

latter shall inform the People of Rome by a special announcement; he shall notify the Cardinal Archpriest of the Vatican Basilica; he shall take possession of the Apostolic Palace in the Vatican and, either in person or through a delegate, of the Palaces of the Lateran and of Castel Gandolfo, and exercise custody and administration of the same"[143].

In addition, he must "determine, after consulting the heads of the three Orders of Cardinals, all matters concerning the Pope's burial, unless during his lifetime the latter had made known his wishes in this regard"[144]. He decides, for example, whether or not it is possible to photograph the pontiff's corpse and when to do so[145].

The Camerlengo decides when the "general congregations" begin to be held; he will set the date in agreement with the first cardinal elector of each of the three orders.

During the Sede Vacante, a commission is formed, composed of the Camerlengo, the (former) Secretary of State and the President of the Pontifical Commission for Vatican City State, to organize the conclave logistically: to arrange the lodging of the cardinal electors in Casa Santa Marta, to prepare the Sistine Chapel for the voting, with special attention to measures to guarantee secrecy. It supervises that the area used during the papal election "and in particular the Sistine Chapel and the areas reserved for liturgical celebrations are to be closed to unauthorized persons"[146].

During the conclave, he keeps a record of the results of each vote; and once the conclave is concluded,

143. Cfr. Apostolic Constitution Universi Dominici Gregis (February 22, 1996) n. 17.
144. Ibid.
145. Cfr. Apostolic Constitution Universi Dominici Gregis (February 22, 1996) n. 30.
146. Cfr. Apostolic Constitution Universi Dominici Gregis (February 22, 1996) n. 43.

he draws up "a document, to be approved also by the three Cardinal Assistants, declaring the result of the voting at each session. This document is to be given to the Pope and will thereafter be kept in a designated archive, enclosed in a sealed envelope, which may be opened by no one unless the Supreme Pontiff gives explicit permission"[147].

In addition, John Paul II entrusted him with another specific mission: "I order each and every Cardinal elector to hand over to the Cardinal Camerlengo or to one of the three Cardinal Assistants any notes which he may have in his possession concerning the results of each ballot. These notes are to be burnt together with the ballots"[148].

Does the Cardinal Camerlengo have access to confidential information about the Holy See?

Yes. The constitution governing the Vatican Curia states that "during the vacancy of the Apostolic See, the Council for the Economy provides the Cardinal Camerlengo of the Holy Roman Church with the most recent consolidated financial statements of the Holy See and the budget for the current year"[149]. Also, "the Secretariat for the Economy furnishes the Cardinal Camerlengo of the Holy Roman Church whatever information may be requested with regard to the financial status of the Holy See"[150]. The Camerlengo has the right to request this information, as well as to "request from all administrations dependent on the Holy See reports on their patrimonial and econom-

147. Ibid.
148. Cfr. Apostolic Constitution Universi Dominici Gregis (February 22, 1996) n. 71.
149. Cfr. Apostolic Constitution "Praedicate Evangelium" (19 March 2022) n. 209 § 2.
150. Cfr. Apostolic Constitution "Praedicate Evangelium" (19 March 2022)n. 218. § 2.

ic status, as well as information on any extraordinary business that may be under way"[151].

What happens if the office of Cardinal Camerlengo becomes vacant?

If there is no Camerlengo at the beginning of the Sede Vacante, the cardinal electors present in Rome must elect as soon as possible and by secret ballot the one who will occupy this office until a new pontiff is elected and appoints another one or confirms the election.

They shall write a name on ballots distributed and collected by the "ceremonieri", assistants to the Master of Papal Liturgical Celebrations. The count will be made in the presence of the three Cardinal Assistants and the secretary of the College of Cardinals. The one who has obtained the majority of votes will automatically have all the faculties of the Camerlengo. In case of a tie, the cardinal belonging to the highest order (order of bishops, priests and deacons) will be elected, and if they belong to the same order, the one who has been created cardinal first[152].

Who takes the place of the Camerlengo before his election?

If there is no Camerlengo, the Dean of the College of Cardinals exercises his functions until one is elected. If the latter is absent or impeded in any way, the Vice-Dean takes his place; and if he is unable to do so, the most senior Cardinal in the order of prec-

151. Cfr. Apostolic Constitution "Praedicate Evangelium" (March 19, 2022) n. 237.
152. Cfr. Apostolic Constitution Universi Dominici Gregis (February 22, 1996) n. 15.

edence. Until a cardinal Camerlengo is appointed, he may make such decisions as circumstances require[153].

How many times has the Cardinal Camerlengo been elected pope?

Only on three occasions. The first was Cosimo Gentile Migliorati, unanimously elected pope in 1404, who became known as Innocent VII. Only eight cardinals participated in that conclave. In 1878, the cardinal Camerlengo Vincenzo Gioacchino Pecci became Pope Leo XIII. The last Camerlengo to be elected pope was Eugenio Pacelli, appointed as such by Pius XI in 1935. A few years later, in 1939, he became Pius XII.

Why does the Major Penitentiary not cease from his office?

Because it is up to him to assist the pope in the remission of canonical sanctions, for example, to pardon persons condemned by excommunication. Specifically, he "grants absolution from censures, dispensations, commutations, validations, remissions and other favours"[154]. If any of the accused repent and request pardon during the period of Sede Vacante, the Catholic Church desires to have the means to grant it immediately.

153. Cfr. Apostolic Constitution Universi Dominici Gregis (February 22, 1996) n. 15.
154. Cfr. Apostolic Constitution "Praedicate Evangelium" (March 19, 2022) n. 191.

Can the Major Penitentiary make all the decisions he deems necessary at his own discretion, during the Sede Vacante?

No. During the Sede Vacante, the Major Penitentiary "continues to carry out the ordinary business within his competence and refers all matters to the College of Cardinals which otherwise would have been referred to the Roman Pontiff"[155].

What happens if at the time of the death of the pope or the beginning of the Sede Vacante there is no Major Penitentiary?

In that case, "the College of Cardinals shall as soon as possible elect the Cardinal who shall hold this office until the election of the new Pope"[156]. They will do so " by a secret vote of all the Cardinal electors present, with the use of ballots distributed and collected by the Masters of Ceremonies. The ballots are then opened in the presence of the Camerlengo and of the three Cardinal Assistants"[157]. Whoever obtains a majority of votes will be automatically elected. "In the case of an equal number of votes, the Cardinal belonging to the higher Order or, if both are in the same Order, the one first created a Cardinal, shall be appointed"[158].

What does the position of cardinal archpriest of a basilica consist of?

The cardinal archpriest of a basilica is the one who

155. Cfr. Apostolic Constitution "Praedicate Evangelium" (March 19, 2022) n. 18.
156. Cfr. Apostolic Constitution Universi Dominici Gregis (February 22, 1996) n. 15.
157. Ibid.
158. Ibid.

presides over the chapter of canons that governs that temple and its patrimony, and the liturgical celebrations that are celebrated in it. The four papal basilicas of St. Peter's, St. Paul's Outside the Walls, St. John Lateran and St. Mary Major have a cardinal archpriest.

What happens if the Vicar General of the Diocese of Rome dies during the Sede Vacante?

In this case, the Vicegerent will exercise this function and, if the Vicegerent is absent, the most senior auxiliary bishop of Rome will do so[159].

Is the activity of the Dicasteries of the Vatican Curia interrupted during the Sede Vacante?

No, the ordinary faculties proper to each Dicastery do not cease, but their presidents do cease and lose executive power over them. When the Sede Vacante begins, all the departments are left in the hands of the second in the hierarchy, that is, the "secretaries", who can make decisions of ordinary administration and use their faculties only "for the granting of favours of lesser importance"[160]. The most serious questions that arise should be reserved exclusively for the future Pontiff.

The law establishes that if these problems cannot wait "(as for example in the case of dispensations which the Supreme Pontiff usually grants in articulo mortis), they can be entrusted by the College of Cardinals to the Cardinal who was Prefect until the Pope's death, or to the Archbishop who was then President,

159. Cfr. Apostolic Constitution Universi Dominici Gregis (February 22, 1996) n. 16.
160. Cfr. Apostolic Constitution Universi Dominici Gregis (February 22, 1996) n. 25.

and to the other Cardinals of the same Dicastery, to whose examination the deceased Supreme Pontiff would probably have entrusted them. In such circumstances, they will be able to decide per modum provisionis, until the election of the Pope, what they judge to be most fitting and appropriate for the preservation and defence of ecclesiastical rights and traditions"[161].

How long have the longest periods of Sede Vacante in history lasted?

Perhaps the longest was that which lasted from 304 to 308. Pope Marcellinus died on October 25, 304. It is unclear when his successor, Marcellus I, was elected, probably between 306 and 308. If he had been elected after July 307, it would have been the longest vacant see in history[162].

The second was the one that took place during the conclave of Viterbo, between 1268 and 1271. That vacant See lasted 33 months.

When John XII resigned in 1415, it was 28 months before there was a new pope validly elected, Martin V in 1417.

Two other vacant sees lasted 27 months. One, between 1292 and 1294, which ended with the election of Celestine V; and another between 1314 and 1316, after which John XXII was elected.

161. Cfr. Apostolic Constitution Universi Dominici Gregis (February 22, 1996) nos. 24 and 25.
162. Cfr. Ambrogio M. Piazzoni, "The Papal Elections. 2000 years of history", Biblioteca Manual Desclée, 2005.

How the mechanics of the conclave has evolved

How was the pope elected before the conclave existed?

Neither the Acts of the Apostles nor Tradition specifies the procedure followed in early Christianity to choose Peter's successor. It is taken for granted that in those early decades, each bishop of Rome personally chose his own successor.

In 336, Pope Mark decided that the new pontiff should be elected by the priests of Rome. These were elections by acclamation, in which the people were somehow given the right to confirm the decision of the priests. From that time are collected many pious legends, - which are only legends. Eusebius of Caesarea relates for example the election of Pope Fabian in the year 236. Fabian was a farmer who was passing through Rome, and stopped to witness the moment when the priests were questioning who might be the next bishop of Rome. Suddenly, however, a dove landed on his head and everyone considered it a sign from God. He was elected pope by acclamation, and immediately ordained priest and bishop.

When the Roman and Byzantine Empire became Christian, the emperor obtained the prerogative of being able to confirm the election of the priests and the people of Rome. Thus, in 557, Emperor Justinian established that without this imperial approval, the elected could not be consecrated bishop of Rome. His successor Justinian II ceded this right to his plenipotentiary, the exarch of Ravenna.

In 769 the right of the laity to refuse election was abolished. But almost a century later, in 862, this right was granted to the nobility of the city of Rome. Precisely to avoid their maneuvers, in 1059, Pope Nicholas II decreed that from then on the only ones who would elect the new pope would be the cardinal bishops, and authorized that among them there would be non-Roman persons. In any case, he maintained the measure that the Roman clergy and the Catholics of the Eternal City should approve the decision.

It is said that Gelasius II (1118) was the first pope elected at a meeting in a secret place closed to the public to avoid outside interference. It was the monastery of San Sebastiano on the Palatine Hill in Rome.

The Lateran Council of 1179 stipulated that two-thirds of the votes of the cardinals were required to be elected pope, and this tradition continues today.

When was the first conclave in history?

Between 1198 and 1268 the cardinals carried out the election in "protected" places. But the conclave was not officially instituted until Gregory X promulgated in 1274 the "Ubi Periculum", which designed it according to a scheme very similar to the present one. According to this criterion, the first conclave would have been held in Arezzo in 1276.

In 1274, Gregory X established that it would be necessary to wait ten days after the death of the pontiff to begin the conclave, that the electors should be shut in "under lock and key" and that their food ration would be reduced every four days until a new pontiff was appointed (from the third day, only one meal and, from the eighth, bread and water). The norms were only applied in the successive election, then they were abolished. Celestine V reintroduced them in 1292, after another conclave that lasted two years and three months. Some of these measures changed again, but the concept of the conclave as an isolated place is maintained to this day.

In 1621, Gregory XV established that there would be three ways to designate the pope: by secret ballot, by acclamation, and by appointing "compromisarii" or delegates.

Throughout the twentieth century, several popes have updated the norms. In 1904, Pius X abolished the right of veto held by the Catholic monarchs of Spain, France, and the Austro-Hungarian Empire. In his own conclave, Emperor Franz Joseph I of Austria had forbidden the election of Cardinal Mariano Rampolla del Tindaro, who was the great favorite.

In 1970, Paul VI established that cardinals lose their right to vote when they reach the age of eighty and, in 1975, in his decree "Romano Pontifici Eligendo", that the number of electors should not exceed 120.

John Paul II, in 1996, eliminated the possibility of electing a new pope by acclamation or by "compromisarii" and ordered the construction of a hotel to accommodate the cardinals during the conclave. Until then, in the conclaves held in the Vatican, they slept in uncomfortable rooms separated by partitions in corridors and halls of the Apostolic Palace, the windows were covered and apparently they could not go outside under any circumstances.

Benedict XVI established in 2007 that, in order to be elected, no matter what two thirds of the votes would be necessary, or two thirds plus one. He also authorized the cardinals to bring forward the start of the conclave if all have arrived in Rome to be able to vote and are in agreement.

Why is it called a "conclave"?

The name "conclave" refers to the idea that the cardinals would lock themselves in a place inaccessible to others, to protect them from external pressures.

In 1059, Pope Nicholas II established that only "cardinal bishops" could participate in the papal election, to avoid interference from the emperor and the nobles. He also established that the pope had to be elected unanimously. This conditioned the duration of the papal elections, which were very long, and made extreme measures necessary to accelerate the result.

It is said that Gelasius II (1118) was the first pope elected in a vote held in a secret place closed to the public to avoid outside interference. It was the monastery of San Sebastiano on the Palatine Hill in Rome.

But the first "conclave" in which the cardinals were locked under lock and key to speed up the election was in Perugia, in 1216, when Honorius III was elected on August 24, 1216.

Sometimes it was the civil authorities themselves who imprisoned them to force the election. In 1241, after the death of Gregory IX, the cardinals could not reach an agreement on the new pope because they were divided between supporters and opponents of

Emperor Frederick II. At that time the College of Cardinals consisted of twelve cardinals, ten of whom were present and two of whom were prisoners in the hands of the emperor. Tired of waiting, the senator of Rome, Matteo Rosso Orsini, ordered that they be locked up ("cum clavis") in the ruins of the old palace of the Septizonio, located on the Palatine Hill in Rome, under precarious hygienic conditions. In a few days, they reached an agreement and elected Celestine IV, who died 16 days later, as pope. It took another two years to elect a new pope.

What has been the longest conclave in history?

The longest papal election in history lasted 34 months, almost three years (1268-1271). The conclave was divided between the cardinals who responded to the pressures of the kings of Naples and Sicily, who represented the interests of France, and the Italian cardinals, who obeyed the Germanic Empire. The conclave was so long that 19 cardinals began it and during the process three of them died. After a year of failed attempts, they were confined in the Papal Palace of Viterbo and the authorities sealed the doors so that they would be incommunicado and could not communicate with the rulers. Since they could not make up their minds, the magistrates of this city increased the pressure and rationed their food, thus forcing them to choose a pontiff if they did not want to starve to death. They even began to remove their roofs so that they would be at the mercy of the weather.

The new pope, Gregory X, wanted to avoid a repetition of what had happened and in 1274, during the Second Council of Lyons, he reformed the norms of the papal election. With the bull "Ubi periculum",

"In case of danger", he prohibited delaying the election of a new pope and established that the conclave would begin ten days after the death of the pontiff in the same city where he died, that the electors should be locked in "with a key", that they would see their food ration reduced every four days until a new pontiff was appointed (from the third day, a single meal and, from the eighth, bread and water), and that their income would be interrupted for the duration of the conclave. These norms were only applied in the successive election, then they were abolished. Celestine V reintroduced them in 1292, after another excessive conclave that lasted two years and three months.

Is it true that during a conclave they removed the ceiling to put pressure on the cardinals?

True, but it was not in the Sistine Chapel, but in the Papal Palace in Viterbo. It was the longest conclave in history. It was the year 1268 and Pope Clement IV had just died. To elect a successor, 19 cardinals went to that city. Three years passed, during which time three of them died, and they were unable to reach an agreement. They were divided between the cardinals who defended the interests of France and those who defended the interests of the Germanic Empire. At the same time, family and personal rivalries divided them into four other factions.

When they arrived in the city in November 1268, the population was initially happy because each cardinal arrived accompanied by a court of about 300 people and this meant work and income for the city. But after almost two years, they grew tired.

On June 1, 1270, the head of the guard, Captain Raniero Gatti and Governor Alberto di Montebuono took the initiative. With the idea of isolating the cardinals from external pressures and speeding up the election, they closed the city gates and locked the cardinals in a room of the "Palace of the Popes". Later they opted to cut down on food and even began to open the roof to leave them out in the open. The idea had come from one of the cardinals who complained that in those circumstances the Holy Spirit could not get through the roof. In the absence of a roof, the cardinals built tents with their coats and staffs, and the floor of the old hall retains the holes over which they built them.

What had happened was recorded on a parchment that is preserved with a message from the cardinals to the civil authorities in which they beg for the door to be opened because one of the cardinals was dying and asked to die outside the conclave. It is signed in Viterbo, in the "Palace without a roof". The reality is that after three weeks, around June 21, they were allowed to stay in other rooms of the palace, with a roof.

It was another year before the election was concluded. On September 1, they agreed to appoint a delegation of six cardinals to designate a new pope. That same day they elected as pontiff a deacon, Theobald Visconti, who at the time was in Acre (present-day Israel), and who did not arrive in Viterbo to accept the election until six months later, on March 2, 1272. He decided to call himself Gregory X. One of his first measures was to modify the law of the conclave so that there would be no repetition of what had happened.

What document currently indicates the norms for the election of the Pope?

It is currently guided by the Apostolic Constitution "Universi Dominici Gregis", "Of the whole flock of the Lord", published by John Paul II on February 22, 1996, feast of the Chair of St. Peter the Apostle and eighteenth year of his pontificate. That document has been modified twice by Benedict XVI, once on June 11, 2007 and again on February 22, 2013. Francis modified some secondary points with the apostolic constitution "Praedicate Evangelium" of March 19, 2022, on the government of the Curia.

What legislation on papal election was being followed up to that time?

The current document is a 1996 law. Until then, the norm in force was the apostolic constitution "Romano Pontifici Eligendo" promulgated by Paul VI in 1975.

The truth is that almost all the pontiffs of the 20th and 21st centuries have modified the norms regarding the conclave. John Paul II elaborated the norms based on those established by his predecessors Pius X in 1904[163], Pius XI in 1922 and 1935[164], Pius XII in 1945[165], John XXIII in 1962[166], and Paul VI in 1967, 1970 and 1975[167].

163. Cfr. Const. ap. Vacante Sede Apostolica (25 December 1904): Pii X Pontificis Maximi Acta, III (1908), 239-288.
164. Cfr. Motu proprio Cum Proxime (1 March 1922): AAS 14 (1922), 145-146; Ap. Const. Quae divinitus (25 March 1935): AAS 27 (1935), 97-113.
165. Cfr. Apostolic Constitution Vacantis Apostolicae Sedis (8 December 1945): AAS 38 (1946), 65-99.
166. Cfr. Motu proprio Summi Pontificis electio (5 September 1962): AAS 54 (1962), 632-640.
167. Cfr. Const. ap. Regimini Ecclesiae universae (15 August 1967): AAS 59 (1967), 885-928; Motu proprio Ingravescentem aetatem (21 November 1970): AAS 62 (1970), 810-813; Const. ap. Romano Pontifici Eligendo (1 October 1975): AAS 67 (1975), 609-645.

Did Benedict XVI modify the rules of the conclave established by John Paul II?

Benedict XVI modified it twice. In 2007 he reintroduced the provision that the new pope needed no matter what two-thirds of the votes to be elected. John Paul II had established an exception to this rule, and Benedict XVI decided to remove it because he feared that in the future it would condition the freedom of voters[168].

According to John Paul II, if after ten days, which amounted to 26 or 27 ballots, no candidate reached two-thirds of the votes, an absolute majority of the votes would be sufficient[169]. Benedict eliminated it and established that in that case the cardinal electors should choose between the two most voted candidates, and that no matter what to be elected it was necessary to receive two thirds of the support of the cardinal electors present.

Years later, on February 22, 2013, six days before his resignation took effect, Benedict XVI introduced new changes. Among other things, he clarified some expressions of the rules and allowed the cardinals to bring forward the beginning of the voting if all the electors are in Rome, or to delay it up to a maximum of 20 days from the beginning of the Sede Vacante.

The final text would be this:

"I furthermore decree that, from the moment when the Apostolic See is lawfully vacant, fifteen full days must elapse before the Conclave begins, in order to

168. Cfr. Motu Proprio "De aliquibus mutationibus in normis de electione Romani Pontificis" with which the Holy Father Benedict XVI reestablishes the traditional norm regarding the majority required for the election of the Supreme Pontiff (June 11, 2007).
169. Cfr. Apostolic Constitution Universi Dominici Gregis (February 22, 1996) N. 75.

await those who are absent; nonetheless, the College of Cardinals is granted the faculty to move forward the start of the Conclave if it is clear that all the Cardinal electors are present; they can also defer, for serious reasons, the beginning of the election for a few days more. But when a maximum of twenty days have elapsed from the beginning of the vacancy of the See, all the Cardinal electors present are obliged to proceed to the election"[170].

Since when did a two-thirds majority become necessary to elect the pope?

The decision dates back almost nine hundred years. In 1059, Pope Nicholas II established that the new pope had to be elected unanimously, which greatly lengthened the duration of the conclaves. A century later, in 1179, the Third Lateran Council promulgated the canon "Licet de evitanda discordia" ("To avoid discord"), which established that two-thirds of the votes were sufficient.

170. Apostolic Letter in the form of "Motu Proprio" of Benedict XVI "Normas nonnullas" on some modifications to the norms concerning the election of the Roman Pontiff (February 22, 2013).

Assemblies of Cardinals

How do the cardinals know the rules of the conclave?

The law on the Sede Vacante establishes that at the first "General Congregations" each cardinal should receive a copy of the Apostolic Constitution "Universi Dominici Gregis" and be given the possibility of proposing any questions that may arise regarding the meaning of the norms and their fulfillment. The law advises the cardinals to read also what refers to the period of Sede Vacante and not only what refers to the conclave[171].

How do you prepare for the papal election?

With the "General Congregations" or plenary assemblies of cardinals. Although during these they make operative decisions, for example about the pope's funeral or the date of the conclave, as soon as possible they focus on exchanging impressions about the situation of the Church and the profile that the next pope should have.

All Cardinals not legitimately impeded are obliged to participate in these meetings, although those over

171. Cfr. Apostolic Constitution Universi Dominici Gregis (22 February 1996) n. 12.

80 years of age, if they so desire, are dispensed.

What are "General Congregations"?

This is the name given to the plenary assemblies of cardinals, held behind closed doors during the Sede Vacante, to make decisions on urgent matters of the Church's life and to exchange impressions on the profile of the next pope.

They will begin "on the day which shall be fixed by the Camerlengo of Holy Roman Church and the senior Cardinal of each of the three Orders among the electors"[172]. They are held practically every day until the new pontiff is elected. They can be of two types: "preparatory" and assemblies of cardinal electors[173]. The preparatory ones are held before the conclave, and the others during the conclave.

All cardinals who are not legitimately impeded, as soon as they are informed of the vacancy of the See, are obliged to participate[174]. In practice, those over 80 years of age may not participate if they prefer to abstain. The law even regulates how they should dress: ordinary black cassock, with a red border and sash, skullcap, pectoral cross and ring.

At their meetings, they deal with "more important matters"[175]. In addition to exchanging impressions on the profile of the next pope, each cardinal "expresses his views on possible problems, asks for explanations in case of doubt and makes suggestions"[176]. Decisions on important matters are made by secret ballot and

172. Cfr. Apostolic Constitution Universi Dominici Gregis (22 February 1996) n. 11.
173. Ibid.
174. Cfr. Universi Dominici Gregis, n. 7.
175. Ibid.

require an absolute majority, that is, half plus one. They have the power to change what the Camerlengo and his three cardinal councilors have established in a "particular congregation," but only by a majority vote.

They are presided over by the Cardinal Dean. If he is over 80 years of age, from the time the conclave begins and the doors of the Sistine Chapel close, the vice-dean cardinal presides, or, if he is also unable to enter, the most senior cardinal elector according to the usual order of precedence[177]. This order is calculated both according to the seniority of the appointment and the order to which the cardinal belongs. Precedence is given to the order of bishops over that of presbyters; and to that of presbyters over that of deacons.

Where are the "General Congregations" held?

The norm that regulates the Sede Vacante establishes that "they will take place in the Vatican Apostolic Palace or, if circumstances require it, in another more opportune place in the judgment of the Cardinals themselves"[178]. After the death of John Paul II and also after the resignation of Benedict XVI, most of them were not held in the Apostolic Palace but in the "New Hall of the Synod", which is in the large audience hall complex, the "Paul VI Hall".

176. Cfr. Universi Dominici Gregis, n. 11.
177. Cfr. Apostolic Constitution Universi Dominici Gregis (22 February 1996) n. 9.
178. Ibid.

Who presides and directs the "General Congregations"?

The Cardinal Dean presides over them, but if he is "absent or lawfully impeded, the Subdean"[179].

If none of them has the right to enter the conclave, during that phase of the election "the senior Cardinal elector, according to the customary order of precedence"[180]. This order is calculated according to both seniority and the order to which the cardinal belongs. Precedence is given to the order of bishops over that of presbyters; and to that of presbyters over that of deacons.

How are decisions made in the "General Congregations"?

For the most important issues, the participants do not vote by word of mouth but by secret ballot. This ensures that they can speak freely[181].

How many "General Congregations" should be held?

Once they begin, "General Congregations" should be held every day during the Sede Vacante, including the day of the pontiff's funeral. The key is to allow the Cardinal Camerlengo to hear "the opinion of the College and communicate whatever is considered necessary or appropriate, while the individual Cardinals can express their views on possible problems, ask for explanations in case of doubt and make suggestions"[182].

179. Ibid.
180. Ibid.
181. Cfr. Apostolic Constitution Universi Dominici Gregis (22 February 1996) n. 10.
182. Cfr. Apostolic Constitution Universi Dominici Gregis (22 February 1996) n. 11.

The "General Congregations" are also called "preparatory" when they precede the beginning of the election[183]; and "assemblies of cardinal electors" when they are held during the conclave.

Must the cardinals keep secret the matters dealt with in the "General Congregations"?

Depends. As cardinals join the General Congregations they must "swear an oath to observe the prescriptions contained in the Apostolic Constitution 'Universi Dominici Gregis' and to maintain secrecy" "with regard to all matters in any way related to the election of the Roman Pontiff or those which, by their very nature, during the vacancy of the Apostolic See, call for the same secrecy"[184]. Naturally, the same degree of secrecy is not required of them for ordinary matters that are not related to the papal election, although they must keep the natural discretion.

What is the text of the secrecy oath?

First, the cardinal dean, or whoever presides over the congregation, will read aloud in the presence and on behalf of all:

> *"We, the Cardinals of Holy Roman Church, of the Order of Bishops, of Priests and of Deacons, promise, pledge and swear, as a body and individually, to observe exactly and faithfully all the norms contained in the Apostolic Constitution Universi Dominici Gregis of the Supreme Pontiff John Paul II, and to maintain rigorous secrecy with regard to all matters in any*

183. Ibid.
184. Ibid.

way related to the election of the Roman Pontiff or those which, by their very nature, during the vacancy of the Apostolic See, call for the same secrecy".

Then, each Cardinal adds:

"And I, N. Cardinal N., so promise, pledge and swear".

And placing his hand on the Gospels, he will say:

"So help me God and these Holy Gospels which I now touch with my hand".

This oath must be taken by all cardinals and should therefore be repeated each time a new cardinal joins the meetings[185].

What are the most urgent decisions to be made in the "General Congregations"?

The law asks them to make decisions as soon as possible on some issues, especially "regarding the beginning of the election"[186]. Specifically they shall:

a) establish the day, hour and manner in which the body of the deceased Pope shall be brought to the Vatican Basilica in order to be exposed for the homage of the faithful;

b) make all necessary arrangements for the funeral rites of the deceased Pope, to be celebrated for nine consecutive days, and determining when they are to begin in such a way that burial will take place, except for special reasons, between the fourth and sixth day after death;

185. Ibid.
186. Cfr. Apostolic Constitution Universi Dominici Gregis (February 22, 1996) n. 13.

c) request the Commission, made up of the Cardinal Camerlengo and the Cardinals who had formerly held the offices of Secretary of State and President of the Pontifical Commission for Vatican City State, to appropriate arrange both the premises of the Casa Santa Marta for the proper accommodation of the Cardinal electors and suitable rooms for those providing assistance during the conclave, and that all necessary arrangements are made to prepare the Sistine Chapel so that the election process can be carried out in a smooth and orderly manner and with maximum discretion;

d) entrust to two ecclesiastics known for their sound doctrine, wisdom and moral authority the task of presenting to the Cardinals two well-prepared meditations on the problems facing the Church at the time and on the need for careful discernment in choosing the new Pope; at the same time, they shall fix the day and the time when the first of these meditations is to be given;

e) approve - at the proposal of the Administration of the Apostolic See or, within its competence, of the Governorate of Vatican City State - expenses incurred from the death of the Pope until the election of his successor;

f) read any documents left by the deceased Pope for the College of Cardinals;

g) arrange for the destruction of the Fisherman's Ring and of the lead seal with which Apostolic Letters are dispatched;

h) make provision for the assignment of rooms by lot to the Cardinal electors;

i) set the day and hour of the beginning of the voting process.

What is the "Particular Congregation"?

This is the assembly that is responsible for making decisions on ordinary matters, and for submitting important questions to the General Congregation. It is presided over by the Cardinal Camerlengo and has three other cardinal electors who are already in Rome; one of them is the cardinal coordinator of the Council for the Economy[187], and the other two will be chosen by lot and renewed every three days.

Its decisions can only be revoked by motions passed by majority in a "General Congregation". Since its members are renewed every three days, a new "particular Congregation" cannot revoke, modify or grant what has been decided, resolved or denied in a previous "particular Congregation"[188].

187. Cfr. Apostolic Constitution "Praedicate Evangelium" (March 19, 2022) n. 235 § 3.
188. Cfr. Apostolic Constitution "Praedicate Evangelium" (March 19, 2022) n. 8.

Who can elect the new pope

Who chooses the new pope?

He is elected by the "cardinal electors", that is, those who on the day of the beginning of the Sede Vacante are less than 80 years old. The norm establishes: "The right to elect the Roman Pontiff belongs exclusively to the Cardinals of Holy Roman Church, with the exception of those who have reached their eightieth birthday before the day of the Roman Pontiff's death or the day when the Apostolic See becomes vacant"[189]. Explicitly, the "Universi Dominici Gregis" establishes that "the right of active election by any other ecclesiastical dignitary or the intervention of any lay power of whatsoever grade or order is absolutely excluded"[190].

What other people can vote in the papal election, apart from cardinal electors?

No one else may intervene, even if they have high ecclesiastical, moral or political dignity. Only cardinal electors may participate. "The right of active election by any other ecclesiastical dignitary or the intervention of any lay power of whatsoever grade or order is

189. Cfr. Apostolic Constitution Universi Dominici Gregis (February 22, 1996) n. 15.
190. Ibid.

absolutely excluded"[191].

Is there any conclave in which someone who was not a cardinal was allowed to vote?

Only in one, in 1417. At that time there were three popes at the same time. To resolve the question, at the Council of Constance, all the cardinals and six bishops from each of the five great Catholic nations were allowed to vote as "deputies of the council". The nations were England, France, Germany, Italy and Spain.

Can any civil government, political party, world leader, multilateral organization, business, religious order, Catholic movement or organization request that a specific candidate not be elected?

No, no candidate can be vetoed.

When John Paul II prepared the norms that regulate the conclave, he put in place the means to prevent interference in the election of the Pope. Therefore, he established that those who accept "under any pretext whatsoever, from any civil authority whatsoever, the task of proposing the veto or the so-called exclusiva, even under the guise of a simple desire"[192]; or who manifest it "to the entire electoral body assembled together or to individual electors, in writing or by word of mouth, either directly and personally or indirectly and through others, both before the election begins and for its duration"[193] would be auto-

191. Cfr. Apostolic Constitution Universi Dominici Gregis (February 22, 1996) n. 33.
192. Cfr. Apostolic Constitution Universi Dominici Gregis (February 22, 1996) n. 80.
193. Ibid.

matically excommunicated.

The pontiff extended this prohibition "to all possible forms of interference, opposition and suggestion whereby secular authorities of whatever order and degree, or any individual or group, might attempt to exercise influence on the election of the Pope".

John Paul II also asked the cardinal electors not to allow themselves to be influenced "by the interference of persons in authority or by pressure groups, by the suggestions of the mass media, or by force, fear or the pursuit of popularity"[194].

In 2013, a few days after the announcement of Benedict XVI's resignation, but before the Sede Vacante came into effect, the Vatican Secretariat of State publicly denounced attempts to "condition" the cardinals, in view of the conclave, with the dissemination of "often unverified, unverifiable or completely false news stories, that cause serious damage to persons and institutions"[195].

What is the 'Ius exclusivæ'?

This is the so-called "right of exclusion", the right to papal veto reserved to some Catholic monarchs of Europe. For example, during the conclave of 1830-1831, Spanish Cardinal Juan Francisco Marco y Catalán reported that King Ferdinand VII vetoed the election of the former nuncio to Madrid, Giacomo Giustiniani. In the conclave of 1903, Cardinal Mariano Rampolla was vetoed by Emperor Franz Joseph I of Austria-Hungary. It was the last time this privilege was used.

194. Cfr. Apostolic Constitution Universi Dominici Gregis (February 22, 1996) n. 83.
195. Communiqué of the Vatican Secretariat of State, February 23, 2013.

If the pope dies during an Ecumenical Council or a Synod of Bishops, could the attendees participate in the election, even if they were not cardinals?

No, in no case could they participate. Only cardinal electors may participate in the election.

What happens if the pope dies or resigns during a Council or Synod of Bishops?

In case of papal death or resignation, "a Council or Synod of Bishops, at whatever point they have reached, must be considered immediately suspended "ipso iure" ("by the law itself"), once notification is received of the vacancy of the Apostolic See. Therefore without any delay all meetings, congregations or sessions must be interrupted, and the preparation of any decrees or canons, together with the promulgation of those already confirmed, must be suspended, under pain of nullity of the same. Neither the Council nor the Synod can continue for any reason, even though it be most serious or worthy of special mention, until the new Pope, canonically elected, orders their resumption or continuation"[196].

Can any cardinal be excluded who meets the requirements to be an elector?

No, no cardinal elector can be excluded from the conclave for any reason or pretext. However, a cardinal elector can renounce the right to participate if they are hindered by "grave impediment, which however must be recognized as such by the College of Cardinals"[197].

196. Cfr. Apostolic Constitution Universi Dominici Gregis (February 22, 1996) n. 34.

On the other hand, "cardinals who have been canonically deposed or who with the consent of the Roman Pontiff have renounced the cardinalate do not have this right. Moreover, during the Sede Vacante the College of Cardinals cannot readmit or rehabilitate them"[198].

Can cardinals who have been created and published in Consistory, but have not been able to participate in the consistory in which the biretta was given, nor the ring, be electors?

If a cardinal has not been able to go to the consistory to personally receive the ring and biretta, his appointment is considered valid in any case, and therefore, he may participate.

Can those whom the pope has said he would make cardinals, but has not been able to officially appoint because the consistory has not been held, enter the conclave?

If the Pope announces the names of the new cardinals, but the consistory is not held, they cannot participate in the conclave, as they are not technically cardinals[199].

197. Cfr. Apostolic Constitution Universi Dominici Gregis (February 22, 1996) n. 35 and 38.
198. Cfr. Apostolic Constitution Universi Dominici Gregis (February 22, 1996) n. 36.
199. Ibid.

Can a cardinal who has resigned or been deposed by the pope enter the conclave?

No, he will not be able to participate in the conclave if he has resigned or has been deposed by the pope. In addition, the College of Cardinals does not have the power to reinstate him[200].

Are all cardinal electors obliged to attend the Conclave?

Yes, all cardinal electors must participate, "unless they are hindered by sickness or by some other grave impediment, which however must be recognized as such by the College of Cardinals"[201].

In the 2005 conclave, there were two cardinal electors who could not participate for health reasons, Adolfo Antonio Suárez Rivera, archbishop emeritus of Monterrey (Mexico), and Jaime Lachica Sin, archbishop emeritus of Manila (Philippines). Two other cardinals declined to participate in the 2013 conclave: Jesuit Julius Riyadi Darmaatmadja, archbishop emeritus of Jakarta, due to health issues; and Scotsman Keith Michael Patrick O'Brien, archbishop emeritus of Edinburgh, accused of inappropriate behavior with adults[202].

How much time do the cardinals have to arrive in Rome in time for the conclave?

When they have notice of the beginning of the Sede Vacante, the cardinals should travel as soon as

200. Ibid.
201. Cfr. Apostolic Constitution Universi Dominici Gregis (February 22, 1996) n. 38.
202. Two years later, on March 20, 2015, Keith Michael Patrick O'Brien definitively renounced all rights and prerogatives attached to the cardinalate.

possible to Rome. The electors will wait for the absentees fifteen full days from the death or resignation of the pope before beginning the conclave. No matter what, the conclave should begin no later than twenty days after the beginning of the Sede Vacante[203].

Interestingly, according to the treaty regulating relations between the Holy See and Italy, Italy "will take special care that the free passage and access of Cardinals to the Vatican through Italian territory is not hindered, nor that the personal freedom of the Cardinals is prevented or limited"[204]. The rule also applies if the conclave is held in another city in Italy[205].

Can a cardinal who arrives in Rome when the election process has already begun be admitted to the conclave?

Yes. In the event that a cardinal elector arrives in Rome and the conclave has begun but the new pontiff has not been elected, he has the right "to be allowed to take part in the election at the stage which it has reached"[206].

What happens if a cardinal elector refuses to enter the conclave or, once it has begun, leaves without just cause?

For the purposes of the validity of the election, nothing changes if any of the cardinal electors leaves without just cause. The rest of the cardinal electors will continue with the conclave, without waiting for him or readmitting him again.

203. Cfr. Apostolic Constitution Universi Dominici Gregis (February 22, 1996) n. 37.
204. Cfr. Lateran Treaty, February 19, 1929, art. 21.
205. Ibid.
206. Cfr. Apostolic Constitution Universi Dominici Gregis (February 22, 1996) n. 39.

What is done if a cardinal has to leave the conclave for reasons of illness?

In the event that he leaves the conclave for health reasons, such as an illness diagnosed "under oath by doctors and confirmed by the majority of the electors", when he recovers he can be readmitted to the Sistine Chapel[207]. In that case, "the election can proceed without asking for his vote; if however he desires to return to the place of the election, once his health is restored or even before, he must be readmitted"[208]. There must be a consensus that he leaves the conclave for a just cause and that he can be readmitted without danger of interference.

What is to be done if a cardinal has to leave for some serious cause recognized by the majority of the electors?

The law regulating the conclave states that "if a Cardinal elector leaves Vatican City for some grave reason, acknowledged as such by the majority of the electors, he can return, in order once again to take part in the election"[209]. It is important that the majority of the electors consider the reason for the absence to be a "grave reason". In any case, in his absence the voting continues, and it is not necessary to wait for him to elect a new pope.

Can sick cardinal electors participate in the conclave and vote?

Sick cardinal electors will be able to attend the con-

207. Cfr. Apostolic Constitution Universi Dominici Gregis (February 22, 1996) n. 40.
208. Ibid.
209. Ibid.

clave and stay at Casa Santa Marta, and if they wish, even vote without leaving their room. Moreover, if they need a nurse to accompany them, "arrangements must be made to provide suitable accommodation for the nurse". Naturally, the assistant will not enter into the voting. It is up to the "particular congregation" to verify the need and approve the eventual presence of the nurse[210].

What is the maximum number of "cardinal electors"?

Paul VI established that there should be no more than 120 cardinal electors[211]. John Paul II confirmed this in the Apostolic Constitution "Universi Dominici Gregis". But in practice this rule is automatically abrogated when the pope appoints new cardinals and the total number exceeds 120. Both John Paul II and Francis exceeded it on several occasions.

What is the maximum age for cardinal electors?

Paul VI established that cardinals who have reached the age of 80 before the day on which the vacancy of the Apostolic See begins do not participate in the papal election[212]. If they reach the age of 80 during the vacancy or conclave, they may participate in the election.

210. Cfr. Apostolic Constitution Universi Dominici Gregis (February 22, 1996) n. 42.
211. Cfr. Motu proprio Ingravescentem aetatem (21 November 1970), II, 2: AAS 62 (1970), 811; Const. ap. Romano Pontifici Eligendo (1 October 1975), 33: AAS 67 (1975), 622.
212. Cfr. Motu proprio Ingravescentem aetatem (21 November 1970), II, 2: AAS 62 (1970), 811; Const. ap. Romano Pontifici Eligendo (1 October 1975), 33: AAS 67 (1975), 622.

Why can't cardinals over 80 years of age participate?

Paul VI, with the motu proprio "Ingravescentem aetatem" of November 21, 1970, provided that when a cardinal reaches 80 years of age he automatically ceases to be a member of the dicasteries of the Roman Curia and of all the permanent bodies of the Holy See and of the Vatican City State; and that he loses the right to enter a conclave.

John Paul II confirmed this measure in 1996 and explained that "the reason for this provision lies in the desire not to add to the burden of such a venerable age the further burden constituted by the responsibility of choosing the one who will have to lead the flock of Christ in a manner suited to the demands of the times"[213].

What should cardinals over 80 years of age do during the conclave?

The Apostolic Constitution "Universi Dominici Gregis" asks them to act leading "the People of God assembled in the Patriarchal Basilicas of Rome and in other churches in the Dioceses throughout the world, supporting the work of the electors with fervent prayers and supplications to the Holy Spirit and imploring for them the light needed to make their choice before God alone and with concern only for the "salvation of souls, which in the Church must always be the supreme law"[214].

213. Cfr. Apostolic Constitution Universi Dominici Gregis (February 22, 1996) Introduction.
214. Cfr. Apostolic Constitution Universi Dominici Gregis (February 22, 1996) Introduction.

How many cardinals participated in the last conclaves?

In 1903, 62 of the 64 cardinals participated.

In 1914, 57 of the 65 cardinals.

In 1922, 53 of the 60 cardinals.

In 1939, all 62 cardinals participated.

In 1958, 51 of the 53 cardinals.

In 1963, 80 of the 82 cardinals.

In August 1978, 111 of the 114 cardinal electors.

In the October 1978 election, 111 of the 112 cardinal electors.

In 2005, 115 of the 117 cardinal electors.

In that of 2013, also 115 of the 117 cardinal electors.

How should cardinals dress during the conclave?

While for the general congregations during the Sede Vacante they wear the "usual black cassock with piping and the red sash, with skullcap, pectoral cross and ring"[215]; for the voting in the Sistine Chapel they must wear the "choir dress", which in their case is the scarlet cassock and the roquette – a short white tunic worn untucked[216].

215. Cfr. Apostolic Constitution Universi Dominici Gregis (February 22, 1996) n. 7.
216. Cfr. Apostolic Constitution Universi Dominici Gregis (February 22, 1996) n. 50.

Conclave Rules

What is the conclave?

The word has several meanings: technically, it is the assembly of cardinals under the age of 80 that elects the new pope; also, the closed place where the voting takes place; and the procedure used to elect a new pontiff[217].

Literally, "conclave" means "under lock and key" ("cum clavis", in Latin). It refers to the papal election in which the cardinals were shut in under lock and key to speed up their decision and protect them from external pressure.

When is the conclave held?

The conclave is held to elect a new pope, thus every time a pontiff resigns or dies. To allow time for the cardinal electors to arrive in Rome and search for the right candidate, the conclave must begin at least fifteen days after the death or resignation, but no later than twenty days.

217. Cfr. "Sede Apostolica Vacante. Storia - Legislazione - Riti - Luoghi e cose". Ufficio delle Celebrazioni Liturgiche del Sommo Pontefice. Vatican City, 2005.

What is the law that currently sets out the rules of the conclave?

It is the Apostolic Constitution "Universi Dominici Gregis" ("From the whole flock of the Lord"), promulgated by John Paul II on February 22, 1996.

Is a conclave necessary for the papal election?

Yes, it is indispensable. John Paul II recognized in the law regulating the procedure for electing a new bishop of Rome that "theologians and canonists of all times consider this institution (the conclave) as not necessary by its nature for the valid election of the Roman Pontiff", but in spite of this he confirms "its validity in its essential structure"[218]. This means, as the law regulating the Sede Vacante and the election of a new Pope makes clear, that the institution of the conclave has responded to historical needs and moments, but that in the future a different method for the election could be used.

How is the pope elected?

He is elected only and exclusively by secret ballot[219]. And to be elected "at least two thirds of the votes are required, calculated on the basis of the total number of electors present and voting"[220]. "Should it be impossible to divide the number of Cardinals present into three equal parts, for the validity of the election of the Supreme Pontiff one additional vote is

218. Cfr. Apostolic Constitution Universi Dominici Gregis (February 22, 1996) Introduction.
219. Cfr. Apostolic Constitution Universi Dominici Gregis (February 22, 1996) Introduction.
220. Cfr. Apostolic Constitution Universi Dominici Gregis (February 22, 1996) n. 62.

required"[221], that is, two thirds plus one.

Can the cardinals decide on another election mechanism?

No, the cardinals, specifically during the period of Sede Vacante, cannot change the rules. Old election mechanisms, such as the "acclamation" and the "compromise" were abolished with the apostolic constitution "Universi Dominici Gregis" of John Paul II, which established that the pope be elected only by the method of secret ballot[222]. He explained that "this form offers the greatest guarantee of clarity, straightforwardness, simplicity, openness and, above all, an effective and fruitful participation on the part of the Cardinals who, individually and as a group, are called to make up the assembly which elects the Successor of Peter"[223].

What was the form of election by acclamation?

It was a unanimous election of the pope, so much so that from 1562 it was called election by "quasi-inspiration" ("per acclamationem seu inspirationem"). The idea was that during the conclave the cardinal electors proclaimed a person pope, chorally, freely and spontaneously. This possibility has been discarded in the Apostolic Constitution "Universi Dominici Gregis", issued by John Paul II in 1996[224].

221. Ibid.
222. Cfr. Apostolic Constitution Universi Dominici Gregis (February 22, 1996) Introduction.
223. Ibid.
224. Cfr. "Sede Apostolica Vacante. Storia - Legislazione - Riti - Luoghi e cose". Ufficio delle Celebrazioni Liturgiche del Sommo Pontefice. Vatican City, 2005.

Gregory III was elected by acclamation in 731 and Gregory VII in 1073. By "quasi-inspiration" Sixtus V was elected in 1585 and Gregory XV in 1621, who then established that this unanimity had to be confirmed by a written vote[225].

What was the "compromise" form of election?

If some time passed and the cardinals could not reach an agreement, they decided unanimously to delegate the vote to some cardinal electors, at least nine and at most fifteen, so that it was easier to reach consensus[226]. This possibility is not considered in the Apostolic Constitution "Universi Dominici Gregis", issued by John Paul II in 1996, to oblige the cardinals to exercise their own responsibility.

Where should the conclave be held?

In 1274, at the Council of Lyon, it was established that the conclave should take place in the city where the pope had died. Since 1455 this rule was changed, and it was proposed that in principle it should be held in Rome.

Currently, the territory of the conclave, that is, the area reserved for the conversations between cardinal electors and the voting to elect the pope, must be within the territory of the Vatican City State "to ensure (...) the seclusion and resulting concentration which an act so vital to the whole Church requires of

225. Cfr. Ambrogio M. Piazzoni, "The Papal Elections. 2000 years of history", Biblioteca Manual Desclée, 2005.
226. Cfr. "Sede Apostolica Vacante. Storia - Legislazione - Riti - Luoghi e cose". Ufficio delle Celebrazioni Liturgiche del Sommo Pontefice. Vatican City, 2005.

the electors"[227].

During the conclave, the cardinals stay at "Casa Santa Marta" in Vatican territory, although the actual voting takes place in the Sistine Chapel.

Where should the cardinal electors stay?

Before the conclave, that is, during the phase of the General Congregations, they may stay wherever they wish. During the conclave, the cardinal electors must stay within Vatican territory, in "Casa Santa Marta", to protect them from external influences and pressures[228].

What is Casa Santa Marta?

It is the official residence of Pope Francis. It is also known by its Latin name, "Domus Sanctae Marthae". It is a residence for ecclesiastics and guests of the Holy See, located within the Vatican territory, very close to St. Peter's Basilica. John Paul II had it built for the papal elections, as he personally experienced the precariousness of the cardinals' lodgings in the two conclaves of 1978 in which he participated. At that time they slept in cells separated by screens in the corridors and halls of the Apostolic Palace, with very few bathrooms available.

During the conclave, its regular guests leave and only the voting cardinals and their companions use it. Casa Santa Marta has an apartment of honor, 105

227. Cfr. Apostolic Constitution Universi Dominici Gregis (February 22, 1996) Introduction.
228. Cfr. Apostolic Constitution Universi Dominici Gregis (February 22, 1996) n. 42.

rooms with offices, and 26 single rooms. There is also a large chapel dedicated to the Holy Spirit, lounges and a dining room. The structure guarantees both rest and seclusion for those participating in the conclave.

Where did the cardinals sleep during the conclave before the construction of Casa Santa Marta?

Until the conclave in which John Paul II was elected, the cardinals were locked in the Apostolic Palace and did not leave it. To accommodate them, dormitories were "improvised" by separating spaces in the rooms of the palace and its corridors with wooden partitions. The window panes were coated with paint to prevent outside viewers from looking in. Food was stored in the kitchen to serve them. John Paul II realized the physical difficulties for the elderly cardinals, and decided to modify it.

When was the first occasion when cardinals were not isolated in the Apostolic Palace?

The Apostolic Constitution "Universi Dominici Gregis", of 1996, establishes that, although the voting will take place in the Sistine Chapel, which is located in the Apostolic Palace, the cardinals must sleep in "Casa Santa Marta", a residence for ecclesiastics and employees in another area of the Vatican, which is reserved for the cardinals on the occasion of the conclave. The first conclave in which this decision was put into practice was that of April 18-19, 2005. Until then, they slept in makeshift cells in the corridors of the Apostolic Palace, separated by temporary wooden partitions.

In addition to the cardinal electors, are there other people who can stay at Casa Santa Marta during the conclave?

Yes, the people involved in assisting during the conclave will be accommodated in Santa Marta, although they will not be able to watch the voting inside the Sistine Chapel.

These are the secretary of the College of Cardinals, who acts as secretary of the elective assembly, the Master of the Pontifical Liturgical Celebrations, who acts as notary after the election, eight Ceremonieri who assist the Master of the Liturgical Celebrations, two religious attached to the Pontifical Sacristy, one ecclesiastic who will assist in his office the cardinal dean or whoever presides over the conclave in his place[229].

The "Universi Dominici Gregis" also includes among those admitted "a number of priests from the regular clergy for hearing confessions in the different languages, and two medical doctors for possible emergencies"; and "a suitable number of persons to be available for preparing and serving meals and for housekeeping". All of them must receive explicit authorization from the "particular Congregation" formed by the Cardinal Camerlengo and his three cardinal assistants and take an oath to maintain the secrecy of what they witness[230].

Can anyone outside the election process approach the cardinals during the conclave?

The Camerlengo and vice Camerlengo will ensure

229. Cfr. Apostolic Constitution Universi Dominici Gregis (February 22, 1996) n. 46.
230. Ibid.

that no one approaches the cardinal electors during the journey from Casa Santa Marta to the Apostolic Palace.

Until 2022, the task of oversight fell to the "Clerical Prelates of the Chamber", who are the priests of the Apostolic Chamber who assisted the Camerlengo and vice Camerlengo; but the Apostolic Chamber was abolished with the apostolic constitution "Praedicate Evangelium" and replaced de facto with the office of the Camerlengo[231].

During the conclave, can the cardinals communicate with people outside the election process by correspondence, telephone or other means?

No, they cannot. "Cardinal electors are likewise to refrain from receiving or sending messages of any kind outside Vatican City; naturally it is prohibited for any person legitimately present in Vatican City to deliver such messages"[232]. During the conclave, they are forbidden "to receive newspapers or periodicals of any sort, to listen to the radio or to watch television"[233].

From the beginning of the conclave until the identity of the new pope is made public, the cardinal electors "are not to communicate — whether by writing, by telephone or by any other means of communication — with persons outside the area where the election is taking place, except in cases of proven and urgent necessity, duly acknowledged by the Particular

231. Cfr. Apostolic Constitution Universi Dominici Gregis (February 22, 1996), n. 43; and Apostolic Constitution "Praedicate Evangelium" (March 19, 2022), n. 12. Already since 2020, the Pontifical Yearbook 2020, does not include the office of "Prelate Clerics of Chamber".
232. Cfr. Apostolic Constitution Universi Dominici Gregis (February 22, 1996) n. 57.
233. Ibid.

Congregation"[234]. In this case, they should request permission from the Cardinal Camerlengo.

It is usual for conclaves to be very brief, but the norm asks what happens in the case of a prolonged election. Regardless, the law states that "it shall therefore be the duty of the Cardinal electors to make necessary arrangements, before the beginning of the election, for the handling of all non-deferrable official or personal business, so that there will be no need for conversations of this sort to take place"[235] and they can concentrate on the election without the risk of external interference.

The "Particular Congregation" will also assess the alleged "necessity and urgency" if the Cardinals Major Penitentiary, Vicar General for the Diocese of Rome and Archpriest of the Vatican Basilica need to communicate with other persons by reason of their office[236].

Can the cardinals talk to whomever they encounter in their path?

The constitution forbids any "conversation of any sort, by whatever means and for whatever reason" with cardinal electors, to those who happen to encounter them during the election period[237].

234. Cfr. Apostolic Constitution Universi Dominici Gregis (February 22, 1996) n. 44.
235. Cfr. Apostolic Constitution Universi Dominici Gregis (February 22, 1996) n. 56.
236. Ibid.
237. Cfr. Apostolic Constitution Universi Dominici Gregis (February 22, 1996) n. 45.

Can the cardinal electors follow the news during the days of the conclave, by any means of communication?

No. "It is specifically prohibited to the Cardinal electors, for the entire duration of the election, to receive newspapers or periodicals of any sort, to listen to the radio or to watch television"[238]. This also applies to Internet content.

Can cardinal electors communicate with their respective dioceses or archdioceses to discuss pending matters?

No. During the conclave, the cardinal electors must "refrain from written correspondence and from all conversations, including those by telephone or radio, with persons who have not been duly admitted to the buildings set aside for their use". They may do so only for "the most grave and urgent reasons, confirmed by the Particular Congregation of Cardinals"[239]. To avoid this type of communication, they should resolve all personal or office requirements "before the beginning of the election"[240].

Can cardinals send or receive messages?

No, they cannot. The law of the conclave explicitly forbids it[241].

238. Cfr. Apostolic Constitution Universi Dominici Gregis (February 22, 1996) n. 57.
239. Cfr. Apostolic Constitution Universi Dominici Gregis (February 22, 1996) n. 56.
240. Ibid.
241. Cfr. Apostolic Constitution Universi Dominici Gregis (February 22, 1996) n. 57.

And can they receive press, or listen to radio, television or internet programs during the election process?

No, they cannot. They are prohibited from receiving daily and periodical press of any kind, as well as listening to radio programs, watching television broadcasts or consulting social networks[242]. It is understood that information from these media could in one way or another interfere with and condition their vote.

Can cardinals bring their cell phones into the Sistine Chapel during voting?

No, they cannot. The law of the conclave states that "in order that the Cardinal electors may be protected from the indiscretion of others and from possible threats to their independence of judgment and freedom of decision, I absolutely forbid the introduction into the place of the election, under whatsoever pretext, or the use, should they have been introduced, of technical instruments of any kind for the recording, reproducing or transmitting of sound, visual images or writing"[243]. This includes cell phones.

Are the cardinals obliged to keep secret what happens during the conclave?

John Paul II, with the authority of Pontiff, affirms in the apostolic constitution that establishes the rules of the conclave: "I further confirm, by my apostolic authority, the duty of maintaining the strictest secrecy with regard to everything that directly or indirect-

242. Ibid.
243. Cfr. Apostolic Constitution Universi Dominici Gregis (February 22, 1996) n. 61.

ly concerns the election process itself"[244].

Can any rule of the conclave be corrected or modified during the vacancy of the Sede Vacante?

No. It is not possible no matter what to modify the law during the process of Sede Vacante, and, if someone were to make changes, they would be declared null and void. John Paul II explicitly stated that "during the vacancy of the Apostolic See, laws issued by the Roman Pontiffs can in no way be corrected or modified, nor can anything be added or subtracted, nor a dispensation be given even from a part of them, especially with regard to the procedures governing the election of the Supreme Pontiff. Indeed, should anything be done or even attempted against this prescription, by my supreme authority I declare it null and void"[245].

Who can change the rules governing the conclave?

Only a sitting pope can change them.

Can a pope, after announcing his resignation, change these rules?

Once the resignation takes effect and the period of Sede Vacante begins, the resigning pontiff no longer has the governing power to modify the norms regarding papal election. If he were to make changes

244. Cfr. Apostolic Constitution Universi Dominici Gregis (February 22, 1996) Introduction.
245. Cfr. Apostolic Constitution Universi Dominici Gregis (February 22, 1996) n. 4.

once the Sede Vacante period begins, they would not be valid.

During the valid period of his government, before the Sede Vacante takes effect, the resigning pontiff can analyze the circumstances that favor the Church and a better development of the conclave, so with full authority he can legitimately change some elements of the mechanism of papal election. Benedict XVI modified some elements of the rules of the conclave six days before his resignation took effect, in order to give the cardinals the possibility of bringing forward the beginning of the conclave.

In case of resignation of the Supreme Pontiff, can these norms be changed?

No, they cannot be changed even in case of papal resignation. The apostolic constitution "Universi Dominici Gregis" promulgated by John Paul II explains that papal resignation is not sufficient reason to modify the mechanism of election of a new pope. It therefore establishes "that the dispositions concerning everything that precedes the election of the Roman Pontiff and the carrying out of the election itself must be observed in full, even if the vacancy of the Apostolic See should occur as a result of the resignation of the Supreme Pontiff"[246].

246. Cfr. Apostolic Constitution Universi Dominici Gregis (February 22, 1996) n 77.

What happens if the election is carried out differently from the apostolic constitution "Universi Dominici Gregis" or without respecting the established conditions?

In such a case, the election would be considered null and void, without any declaration being required in this regard and without the person supposedly elected having acquired any rights[247].

247. Cfr. Apostolic Constitution Universi Dominici Gregis (February 22, 1996) n 76.

No election campaign

Who are the "papabili"?

They are cardinals in whom public opinion and Vatican observers recognize qualities of governance that could one day lead them to become pope.

Who can be elected pope?

The cardinals must give their vote "to the person, even outside the College of Cardinals, who in their judgment is most suited to govern the universal Church in a fruitful and beneficial way"[248]. It means that any person who meets the conditions to be bishop of Rome can be elected pope. Therefore, he must be a baptized, unmarried male.

In addition, to be appointed bishop it is necessary to be over 35 years old, to have been a priest for at least five years, to have a degree in Theology, Canon Law or Sacred Scripture from an ecclesiastical faculty, and to have a good reputation.

In practice, he is chosen from among the cardinal electors.

248. Cfr. Apostolic Constitution Universi Dominici Gregis (February 22, 1996) n 83.

What criteria should cardinals follow to identify their candidate?

John Paul II, in the law of the conclave, asked them not to let themselves be carried away "by friendship or aversion". Nor "by favour or personal relationships towards anyone" or by external pressures[249]. It is a matter of keeping in mind "solely the glory of God and the good of the Church"[250]. Therefore, they should give their vote "to the person, even outside the College of Cardinals, who in their judgment is most suited to govern the universal Church in a fruitful and beneficial way"[251].

What political tendencies are there within the College of Cardinals?

From experience I can say that the division between conservative and liberal cardinals does not help to understand the reality of what happens in a conclave.

In his book "Conclave", Vaticanist John Allen Jr. identifies three currents of thought among the cardinals who would follow this model[252]:

- The first is that of the conservatives, who consider it a priority to protect the morality and orthodoxy of the faith. They call them the "frontier police", and their priority is to ensure that Christian identity is not contaminated by the ideas of a secularized society. It is a matter of vigilance over practices, rituals and doctrine.

249. Ibid.
250. Ibid.
251. Ibid.
252. Cfr. Allen Jr. John, "Conclave. The Politics, Personalities, and Process of the Next Papal Election", Doubleday. 2002.

- The second is that of those who try to make society assume Christian doctrine. They are called the "Salt of the Earth" party, with the idea that Christian doctrine would give flavor to society. In this there are two sensibilities, one that gives priority to issues such as the defense of life, gay marriage or euthanasia; and another that considers it fundamental to act in areas such as human rights, environmental protection and social justice.

- The third current is "reformist" and works to change the structures of the Church. For example, a more "collegial" or democratic Church. Currently it could correspond to those who defend the female diaconate or exceptions to the discipline of priestly celibacy in remote areas where it is difficult to have a stable priest[253].

Another way to study the tendencies within the conclave is to establish four complementary poles around which pivots the position each cardinal has on how to be pope. In this model, it is fundamental to start from the idea that the cardinals agree that the priority of the future pontiff is evangelization. What divides them is the way to carry it out, the role of the pope and the other priorities.

1) Some think that in order to evangelize society, the priority should be to govern the Church from the inside. Their priorities include clarifying doctrinal or moral questions, taking care of the liturgy so that it conveys a sense of mystery, promoting canonization processes to show the current face of Christianity, denouncing the situation of persecuted Christians, easing the mechanisms of Canon Law in order to solve the abuse crisis, defending the Christian presence

253. The examples are by Javier Martínez-Brocal.

and identity in areas where Catholic institutions traditionally work, such as education or health care.

2) Others think that in order to promote the Church's presence in society, it should focus primarily on the outside world. Thus, they believe that the Church and the Pope must give a concrete response to the difficult situations of the contemporary world and must strive to provide a solution to social injustices. For example, it must invest energy and resources in combating hunger, poverty and misery, countering the environmental crisis, mediating in ongoing conflicts, denouncing injustice, etc.

Neither of these two views consider the other to be wrong and therefore does not oppose it. However, it considers them to be dealing with "secondary" issues.

The other two poles, compatible with both positions, oscillate between intervention and mobilization.

1) There are cardinals who are committed to direct intervention to make their priorities a reality, they advocate an institutional presence of the Church in organizations that work to defend their interests, such as associations of Catholic lawyers, political parties that officially define themselves as Christian, Catholic social aid foundations or confessional media.

One way to intervene directly is, for example, to delimit "non-negotiable principles" for social debate between Bishops' Conferences and governments. These principles would be the right to life, the family based in marriage, the educational freedom of parents and religious freedom.

2) Others consider that the Church's mission is to inspire, to mobilize the free personal initiative of Catholics in social issues. It is a less presential, unpredictable and concrete way, which avoids giving precise indications or asking for accountability. For example, Pope Francis summed it up in the attitude of "initiating processes".

What circumstantial elements influence the election of the new pope?

The first is whether the election occurs after a papal resignation or after a death. In the case of resignation, the reasons for resignation directly influence the profile of the successor that the college of cardinals will seek.

The situation of the world at the very moment when the Vacant See begins is also very relevant. A world at war is not the same as a world moving towards peace. Or a society marked by terrorism of a religious matrix, by a pandemic, by a climate crisis, or by the disintegration of supranational institutions, to give just a few examples.

Naturally, the circumstances of the Church during the Sede Vacante have a great influence. The cardinals must consider the priorities for Catholics: the loss of Christians in a given area, indifference to religious questions, persecution or social discrimination of believers, disorder in the Vatican Curia or in its accounts, the matter of abuses. The key is that the new Bishop of Rome must be able to respond to the challenges facing the Church and the world.

What personal elements will the cardinals look for in their candidates?

The Pope is not a manager or a political leader, but a "father" for billions of people. Therefore, he must be a person of spiritual weight, with the ability to encourage, inspire and transmit hope; he must have a global vision of society and be able to be above ideologies and unite people of different sensibilities; and demonstrate leadership skills to govern the Catholic Church without turning it into an army or a multinational corporation.

He must have the energy to face an exhausting work schedule of meetings, interviews and travel. He must speak Italian to guide the Vatican Curia and be fluent in some of the most important languages.

The Pope is above all a message. He must be a man of faith who embodies that message, a man of prayer who transmits the presence of God. A man whose gestures reflect the goodness of Jesus Christ. A man whose gaze opens horizons and gives hope.

Is it allowed to pay to be elected pope?

No, it is forbidden and is considered a grave sin. It is the sin of "simony". The law of the conclave deals with it in the section "What must be observed or avoided in the election of the Supreme Pontiff". In this regard, the norm calls for vigilance against this "crime" and declares that those who commit it will be automatically excommunicated, although the election cannot be declared invalid for this reason.

"If - God forbid - in the election of the Roman Pontiff the crime of simony were to be perpetrated,

I decree and declare that all those guilty thereof shall incur excommunication latae sententiae ("automatic"). At the same time I remove the nullity or invalidity of the same simoniacal provision, in order that — as was already established by my Predecessors — the validity of the election of the Roman Pontiff may not for this reason be challenged"[254].

What exactly is the sin of "simony"?

It is any act or intention that seeks to buy or sell spiritual goods in exchange for material benefits. It refers for example to ecclesiastical offices, sacraments, relics, prayer promises, grace, ecclesiastical jurisdiction, excommunication, etc.

The term derives from a character named Simon Magus, mentioned in chapter VIII of the book of the Acts of the Apostles[255]. In it it is related that Philip the Evangelist converted to Christianity a certain Simon, a sorcerer of Samaria. When Peter and John arrived in that city, Simon offered them money in exchange for the power to transmit the Holy Spirit, a proposition that both apostles, scandalized, rejected. Peter even said to him: "May your money perish with you, because you thought that you could buy the gift of God with money"[256]. The Church recalls that "simony" is a dishonorable sin, contrary to the word of Jesus Christ. The Gospel of Matthew records that he clearly said, "Without cost you have received; without cost you are to give"[257].

254. Cfr. Apostolic Constitution Universi Dominici Gregis (February 22, 1996) n. 78.
255. Acts of the Apostles 8, 9-24.
256. Acts of the Apostles 8, 20.
257. Matthew 10, 8.

Simony was also condemned in 1139 by the Second Lateran Council and again particularly by the Council of Trent (1545-1563).

Can the cardinals make pacts among themselves, alliances or offer votes for the conclave while the pontiff is alive or has not resigned?

The norms published by John Paul II expressly forbid this[258]. Even if they are cardinals, as long as the pontiff is alive and in office, they cannot "promise vows or make decisions in this regard in private meetings"[259]. This does not prevent them from exchanging impressions about persons qualified to be bishops of Rome.

Can a cardinal make pacts, agreements, promises or commitments of any kind that oblige him to give or deny the vote to one or some cardinals?

No, it cannot. Moreover, the law of the conclave states that "if this should actually happen, even under oath, I decree that such a commitment is null and void and that no one is obliged to observe it"[260]. Moreover, it punishes with 'latae sententiae' (automatic) excommunication those who do so. Naturally, this does not mean that there cannot be exchanges of ideas about the election or about the personality and preparation of a possible candidate.

258. Cfr. Apostolic Constitution Universi Dominici Gregis (February 22, 1996) n. 79.
259. Ibid.
260. Cfr. Apostolic Constitution Universi Dominici Gregis (February 22, 1996) n. 81.

Can a cardinal make promises or propose counter-changes to obtain the vote of other cardinals?

No, he cannot, it is forbidden[261]. In fact, to leave them free if they were elected pope, John Paul II declared these promises null and void, "even if they were made under oath"[262].

What happens if before the election some cardinals commit themselves to each other by making pacts or commitments, which must be fulfilled in case one of them is elected pontiff?

These are invalid commitments. To leave future pontiffs free, John Paul II declared these eventual promises of the cardinals null and void, -"should any in fact be made, even under oath, I also declare null and void"[263].

Can a woman be elected pope?

The cardinals may elect as pope a person who meets the conditions to serve as bishop of Rome. The legislation of the Catholic Church only allows priestly ordination to men; if canonically she cannot be ordained as a priest or bishop, neither can she be a pope.

261. Cfr. Apostolic Constitution Universi Dominici Gregis (February 22, 1996) n. 82.
262. Ibid.
263. Ibid.

Why in the Sistine Chapel

Where should the conclave vote be held?

John Paul II specifically arranged for the voting to be held in the Sistine Chapel, where "the electors can more easily dispose themselves to accept the interior movements of the Holy Spirit"[264], because there "everything is conducive to an awareness of the presence of God, in whose sight each person will one day be judged"[265].

Why is the election of the Pope held in a chapel and not in a lecture hall?

The Vatican norm considers that a chapel is pertinent because the conclave requires a space that allows the fulfillment of juridical formalities and liturgical ceremonies, such as the eventual episcopal ordination of the new pope, if he is not a bishop. This also helps the cardinals to make their decision in the "presence of God"[266], aware of the spiritual repercussions of their decision. The constitution Universi Dominici Gregis recommends that the conclave be held in the Sistine Chapel.

264. Ibid.
265. Ibid.
266. Cfr. Apostolic Constitution Universi Dominici Gregis (February 22, 1996) Introduction.

Why is it done in the Sistine Chapel?

John Paul II arranged for the conclave to be held if possible in the Sistine Chapel because there "everything is conducive to an awareness of the presence of God, in whose sight each person will one day be judged"[267].

On the other hand, on a personal note, John Paul II dedicated a poem to the Sistine Chapel in which he evokes the message that Michelangelo's frescoes convey to the cardinals during the conclave.

"Michelangelo's vision must then speak to them.

"Con-clave": a joint concern for the legacy of the keys of the Kingdom.
They will find themselves between the Beginning and the End,
between the Day of Creation and the Day of Judgment.
It is given to man once to die and after that the judgment!

A final clarity and light.
The clarity of the events -
The clarity of consciences -
It is necessary that during the Conclave, Michelangelo teach them -
Do not forget: Omnia nuda et aperta sunt ante oculos Eius.
You who see all - point to him!
He will point him out..."[268]

The conditions of the Sistine Chapel, located inside the Vatican Apostolic Palace, with no windows

267. Cfr. Apostolic Constitution Universi Dominici Gregis (February 22, 1996) Introduction.
268. Second part of the "Roman Triptych" of John Paul II (2003).

or direct access, make it possible for the cardinals to exchange views on the future of the Church and the profile of the next pope, without outside interference.

Is the conclave a spiritual retreat?

Many liken the conclave to a spiritual retreat in which the cardinals meet and answer a question before God, who among us is most worthy to ensure the guidance of the Church and has the spiritual, pastoral, intellectual and human traits suited to the needs of the world and the Church at this time?

John Paul II emphasized in the law of the conclave "the sacred character of the act" and "the convenience of its taking place in an appropriate place, in which, on the one hand, the liturgical celebrations can be united with the juridical formalities and, on the other, the electors can prepare their spirits to welcome the interior motions of the Holy Spirit". For this reason, he established that the conclave be held in the Sistine Chapel, where "everything is conducive to an awareness of the presence of God, in whose sight each person will one day be judged".

Since when has the conclave been held in the Vatican?

Since 1455, almost all the conclaves have been held in the Vatican Apostolic Palace, although not always in the Sistine Chapel. Only five have been held outside the Vatican: that of 1800 was held in Venice; and those of 1823, 1829, 1830 and 1846 were held in the Quirinal Palace in Rome. Since 1878, all the conclaves have been held in the Vatican.

The advantage of holding it in the Quirinal was that the spaces were better adapted to accommodate the cardinal electors.

Since when is the conclave held in the Sistine Chapel?

The first time a conclave was held in the Sistine Chapel was in 1492. Since then, all have been held there except for five conclaves, one in Venice (1800) and four in the Quirinal Palace in Rome, the current official residence of the President of the Italian Republic and then the seat of the pontiffs. The conclaves of 1823, 1829, 1830 and 1846 were held there.

The conclave has been held in the Vatican Apostolic Palace since 1455.

Why is it called the Sistine Chapel?

It owes its name to the pope who ordered its construction, Sixtus IV, of the Della Rovere family, who ruled the Catholic Church from 1471 to 1484. He wished to have a private chapel on the site of the "Cappella Magna", a medieval fortified hall used for meetings of the papal court. At that time the court had about 200 members and was composed of a college of 20 cardinals, representatives of the religious orders and of the most important Roman families, of the college of cantors, and of a certain number of laymen and servants.

Like St. Peter's Basilica, after the exile to Avignon, the "Cappella Magna" was in poor condition and too large for daily liturgical celebrations. The Pontiff needed a small chapel near his residence. For this reason, its entrance is not at street level but on the upper floors of the Apostolic Palace.

The construction also had to respond to the defensive requirements of two threats that then threatened the pope's government: the Signoria of Florence, ruled by the Medici, with whom the pope was in permanent tension; and the Turks of Mehmed II, who in those years were threatening the eastern coasts of Italy.

He entrusted the project to the architect Baccio Pontelli. Construction began in 1475, the year of the Jubilee proclaimed by Sixtus IV, and was completed in 1483. He himself inaugurated it on August 15, since the Sistine was then dedicated to the Virgin of the Assumption, which is commemorated on that day.

What are the dimensions of the Sistine Chapel?

It measures 40.23 meters long, 13.40 meters wide and 20.70 meters high. Some say that it reproduces the measurements of the great temple of Solomon in Jerusalem, destroyed by the Romans in 70 AD.

Is it used only for the conclave?

No, because the conclave is rarely held. It is generally open to the public and is part of the tour of the Vatican Museums. In addition, the pope celebrates Holy Mass there on special occasions, such as on the feast of the Baptism of the Lord, when he administers this sacrament to babies, children of Vatican employees.

Is it true that it was embellished with Michelangelo's frescoes?

Yes, but not only by Michelangelo. The chapel was initially decorated by the best painters of the fifteenth century. Artists such as Pietro Perugino, Sandro Botticelli, Domenico Ghirlandaio, Cosimo Rosselli, helped by their workshops and by collaborators such as Biagio di Antonio, Bartolomeo della Gatta and Luca Signorelli.

They began the frescoes in 1481 and concluded them in 1482. They go through the life of Moses on the one side, and on the other, the life of Jesus, with episodes that suggest a certain parallelism. In addition, several pontiffs are represented on its four walls. The vault was initially a starry sky, the work of Piermatteo d'Amelia. Once completed, on August 15, 1483 Pope Sixtus IV consecrated it and dedicated it to the Assumption of the Virgin.

Years later, in 1508, Pope Julius II, of the Della Rovere family, reigning from 1503 to 1513, asked Michelangelo to replace the starry sky of the vault with new frescoes. Michelangelo decided to paint scenes from the Old Testament and figures of the prophets and sibyls of the classical world. In the nine central panels there are stories from Genesis: the Creation of the world, the Creation of Adam and Eve, the Original Sin, the Flood and the rebirth of humanity with the family of Noah. On November 1, 1512, Julius II inaugurated these frescoes with a solemn Mass.

In 1522 there was a collapse and two frescoes in the Sistine by Ghirlandaio and Signorelli were destroyed. About fifty years later, during the pontificate of Gregory XIII (1572-1585) they were replaced with frescoes by Hendrik van den Broeck and Matteo da Lecce.

Meanwhile, at the end of 1533, the new pope, Clement VII, of the Medici family, pontiff from 1523 to 1534, commissioned Michelangelo to paint the Last Judgment on the wall on the side of the altar. To do so, Michelangelo had to remove some 15th century frescoes, such as the altarpiece with the Assumed Virgin among the Apostles and the first two episodes of the stories of Moses and Christ, which had been painted by Perugino.

In his "Last Judgment" he depicted the glorious return of Christ at the end of time. The artist began the grandiose work in 1536 during the pontificate of Paul III and completed it five years later, in the autumn of 1541.

Why did they have to restore Michelangelo's frescoes in the 20th century?

The frescoes were blackened and lost their original vivid color due to the passage of time and the use of candles. The directors of the Vatican Museums decided to restore them. The operation lasted from 1979 to 1999. It took more time to restore the frescoes than to realize them.

From what period is the pavement of the Sistine Chapel?

The splendid mosaic pavement, in cosmatesque style, still intact today, dates back to 1400 and follows medieval models.

Is it true that a bomb fell on the Sistine Chapel?

In reality, it was not a bomb but an explosion that took place in 1797 in the powder magazine of the Castel Sant'Angelo, near the Vatican. The impact of the shrapnel reached the Sistine Chapel and destroyed part of the ceiling and the vault painted by Michelangelo. It is the scene of the universal Flood. You can still notice the absence of paint in that area.

Who prepares the Sistine Chapel for the conclave?

The law states that it must be prepared by "trusted personnel who are constantly monitored to ensure that recording and transmission instruments, whether video or audio, are not hidden"[269]. Specifically, this task is carried out by the Vatican department responsible for decoration, called the "Floreria".

For the conclave, the floor is raised so that it is at the same height as the presbytery, the area where the altar is. In this way, the cardinals will not have to climb up and down steps when they go to vote.

Tables are arranged parallel to the wall, in two rows of tables on either side of the chapel. The back row is raised so that all cardinals are always in view.

In 2013, 40 people worked on these tasks. In a statement they explained that the chairs were made of cherry wood and bore the name of each cardinal. They arranged twelve wooden tables, three and three on each side, in two rows, and covered them with a beige and burgundy satin cloth. Before the altar was another table for the urn and also a lectern with the

269. Cfr. "Sede Apostolica Vacante. Storia - Legislazione - Riti - Luoghi e cose". Ufficio delle Celebrazioni Liturgiche del Sommo Pontefice. Vatican City, 2005.

Gospel on which the cardinals would have taken their oath.

Can cameras or recorders be placed inside the Sistine Chapel?

The constitution "Universi Dominici Gregis" requests the Camerlengo to do everything possible to shield what happens during the election, "so that total secrecy may be ensured with regard to everything said or done there in any way pertaining, directly or indirectly, to the election of the Supreme Pontiff"[270].

It is also the responsibility of the College of Cardinals, which acts under the authority and responsibility of the Camerlengo. He himself, with the collaboration of the Substitute of the Secretariat of State, must guarantee "the orderly election and its privacy will be ensured"[271].

The law foresees that "careful and stringent checks must be made, with the help of trustworthy individuals of proven technical ability, in order to ensure that no audiovisual equipment has been secretly installed in these areas for recording and transmission to the outside"[272].

The basic idea is to give the cardinals the freedom to vote for the candidate they consider most suitable, without having to explain their decision or be pressured.

270. Cfr. Apostolic Constitution Universi Dominici Gregis (February 22, 1996) n. 51.
271. Ibid.
272. Ibid.

Does the Sistine Chapel have security cameras and monitoring?

The entire area of the Vatican Museums is monitored by security cameras. However, those in the Sistine Chapel must be switched off during the conclave period and any recording must be prevented.

Can a police force other than the Vatican police guard the conclave area?

Yes. According to the Lateran Treaty, "Italy shall see to it that in its territory around Vatican City no acts are committed which may disturb the meetings of the conclave"[273].

Was there any superstition about the conclave?

The Sistine Chapel has on one of its side walls a fresco by Perugino with the scene of Christ handing the Keys to Peter. Superstition had it that the cardinal whose turn it was to sit in the place under that fresco was the one most likely to be elected. It seems that at least three popes were seated as cardinals under that fresco during their conclaves: Julius II, Clement VII and Paul III.

273. Cfr. Lateran Treaty, February 19, 1929, art. 21.

For how long should Casa Santa Marta, the Sistine Chapel and the areas used for liturgical celebrations be reserved for Cardinals?

These areas will remain closed from the beginning of the election process until the election of the new pontiff is publicly announced or, at the direction of the new pontiff. The key is that the entire territory of Vatican City and the ordinary activity of the Offices located there must be regulated, during this period, in such a way as to ensure the normal development of the papal election and not interfere with it[274].

Are St. Peter's Basilica and the Vatican Museums closed during the conclave?

No. St. Peter's Basilica and the Vatican Museums remain open to the public at their normal hours. Visitors are only advised that the Sistine Chapel area and the annexes used for the conclave are closed to the public.

How long does the conclave last?

It is usually brief. The last ones have not lasted more than five days, although there is no fixed rule. This was the duration of the conclaves of the 20th and 21st centuries:

February 19-20, 1878.
It lasted two days and it took 3 ballots to elect Leo XIII, who was the Camerlengo.

274. Cfr. Apostolic Constitution Universi Dominici Gregis (February 22, 1996) n. 43.

July 31 to August 4, 1903.
It lasted five days and it took 7 ballots to elect Pius X.

August 31 to September 3, 1914.
It lasted four days and it took 10 ballots to elect Benedict XV.

February 2 to 6, 1922.
It lasted five days and it took 14 ballots to elect Pius XI.

March 1 to 2, 1939.
It lasted two days and it took three ballots to elect Pius XII, who was Secretary of State and Cardinal Camerlengo.

October 25-28, 1958.
It lasted four days and it took 11 ballots to elect John XXIII.

June 19-21, 1963.
It lasted three days and it took 6 ballots to elect Paul VI.

August 25-26, 1978.
It lasted two days and it took four ballots to elect John Paul I, who died 33 days later.

October 14-16, 1978.
It lasted three days and it took eight ballots to elect John Paul II.

April 18-19, 2005.
It lasted two days and it took 4 ballots to elect Benedict XVI, who was dean of the College of Cardinals.

March 12-13, 2013.
It lasted two days and it took 5 ballots to elect Francis.

What has been the shortest conclave in history?

Probably that of Pope Julius II, elected on the night between October 31 and November 1, 1503. It lasted only ten hours. Since then, no other pontiff has ever been elected on the first ballot.

The day of the first vote

When should the conclave begin?

In principle, it should begin at least fifteen days after the death of the Pope, and before twenty days have passed. If all the cardinal electors who intend to participate are in Rome and consider it appropriate, they are allowed to advance the date[275]. In 2013, after the resignation of Benedict XVI, they began twelve days after the beginning of the Sede Vacante.

Can the conclave start at any time of the day?

Vatican law suggests that it begin in the morning with the Mass "Pro eligendo Papa", so that in the afternoon the electors can already gather in the Sistine Chapel[276] and if they wish they can begin to vote.

They are summoned to Casa Santa Marta, from where they must leave for St. Peter's Basilica for the Mass "Pro eligendo Papa", ("For the election of the Pope"). Once the ceremony is over, they may no longer leave Vatican territory or come into contact with people outside the election until there is a new bishop of Rome. They may not, among other things,

275. Cfr. Apostolic Constitution Universi Dominici Gregis (February 22, 1996) n. 49.
276. Ibid., and Cfr. Ordo Rituum Conclavis, Year 2000, n. 18.

receive or make phone calls, send text messages or e-mails, or follow the media, to protect themselves from outside influences.

What is the schedule for the conclave?

In 2013, the cardinals followed this schedule during the conclave:

First day

7:00 am.
Transfer of the cardinal electors to Santa Marta. Before ten o'clock in the morning all should be installed there.

10:00 am.
Mass "Pro eligendo Papa" in St. Peter's Basilica.

1:30 pm.
Lunch for the Cardinals at Casa Santa Marta.

3:45 pm.
Transfer from Casa Santa Marta to the Apostolic Palace. They will meet first in the Pauline Chapel.

4:30 pm.
The procession departs from the Pauline Chapel to the Sistine Chapel.

4:45 pm.
Oath of the Cardinals, Extra Omnes and first meditation. They will then decide whether to conduct the first scrutiny. Fumata.

7:30 pm.
Return to Casa Santa Marta.

8:00 pm.
Dinner.

Next days

6:30 am.
Breakfast.

7:45 am.
Transfer from Casa Santa Marta to the Apostolic Palace.

8:15 am.
Mass in the Pauline Chapel.

9:30 am.
First round, two ballots in the Sistine Chapel. Fumata.

12:30 pm.
Return to Casa Santa Marta.

1:00 pm.
Food.

4:00 pm.
Transfer from Casa Santa Marta to the Apostolic Palace.

4:50 pm.
Second round of voting inside the Sistine Chapel. Fumata.

7:15 pm.
Praying Vespers in the Sistine Chapel.

7:30 pm.
Reeturn to Casa Santa Marta.

8:00 pm.
Dinner.

Does the conclave begin in St. Peter's Basilica?

According to the current arrangements, it is proposed that the cardinal electors meet in the morning at St. Peter's Basilica in the Vatican to begin the conclave with a solemn votive Mass "Pro eligendo Papa" ("To pray for the election of the Pope"), so that in the afternoon they can begin voting[277]. The "Universi Dominici Gregis" proposes St. Peter's Basilica but leaves the door open to celebrate this Mass in other places, "should circumstances warrant it"[278].

This mass is usually celebrated by the cardinal dean and the diplomatic corps is invited. The entrance is also open to pilgrims who wish to attend.

Who can participate in the Mass "Pro eligendo Papa"?

It is a Mass concelebrated by all the cardinal electors, to which "other cardinals (non-electors), bishops, priests, deacons, members of institutes of consecrated life and societies of apostolic life, and all the faithful present in Rome are also warmly invited"[279].

277. Cfr. Apostolic Constitution Universi Dominici Gregis (February 22, 1996) n. 49, and Cfr. Ordo Rituum Conclavis, Year 2000, n. 29.
278. Cfr. Apostolic Constitution Universi Dominici Gregis (February 22, 1996) n. 49, and Cfr. Ordo Rituum Conclavis, Year 2000, n. 18.
279. Cfr. Ordo Rituum Conclavis, Year 2000, n. 5.

What are the prayers used in the Mass "Pro eligendo Papa"?

It is a mass to ask God to help them in the election of the Pope. The prayers are these[280]:

Collect prayer

O God, You who as eternal shepherd lead Your flock with ceaseless protecting care, grant Your Church a shepherd who will be pleasing to You with his holiness of character and consecrate himself entirely to the service of Your people. Through Jesus Christ, our Lord.

Prayer over the Offerings

Open, O Lord, the treasures of your mercy and through these sacred gifts that we reverently offer to you, may we rejoice that a shepherd pleasing to Your majesty is set over your Holy Church. Through Jesus Christ, our Lord.

Prayer after Communion

O Lord, You who have renewed us with the sacrament of the Body and Blood of your Son, grant that we may rejoice in the gift of that shepherd who will instruct your people by his virtues and enlighten the minds of the faithful with the truth of the Gospel. Through Jesus Christ, our Lord.

280. Cfr. Ordo Rituum Conclavis, Year 2000.

What should we pay attention to during the Mass "Pro eligendo Papa"?

Apart from the theological and spiritual value of this Mass, the homily delivered by the senior cardinal is very relevant, since it is his last public speech before the election of the new pope. In his homily he usually outlines the profile that in his opinion the next pontiff should have, and the criteria that should guide the cardinals during the electio.

How do cardinals get to the Sistine Chapel?

In the early afternoon, the cardinals depart from Casa Santa Marta to the Vatican Apostolic Palace on foot or in minibuses. They are dressed in the "choir dress", which in the case of the cardinals is the scarlet cassock and the roquette - a short tunic worn untucked.

What should they do before they start voting?

That first afternoon, they meet first in the Pauline Chapel, where the Eucharist will be reserved during all the days of the conclave. It is an important place because the frescoes of the crucified apostle Peter, painted by Michelangelo, remind the cardinals that the new pontiff will also be a martyr.

"When all have assembled the cardinal dean, or if he is absent or legitimately impeded the vice dean or the first cardinal by order and seniority, begins the rite of entrance into conclave"[281], leads prayers in

281. Cfr. Ordo Rituum Conclavis, Year 2000, n. 32.

which all again ask God's help "to do always what He wills"[282], and form the procession.

From there, they all set out together for the Sistine Chapel, the place and venue of the election[283]. They follow the order of precedence, from least to most important. They are preceded by the cross and followed by the Gospel book. They walk responding to the "Litany of the Saints" in which they invoke the help of the great figures in the history of Christianity.

What is the Pauline Chapel?

It is a chapel located inside the Apostolic Palace, which serves as the parish church of the Vatican. It is smaller than the Sistine and is separated from it by the "Sala Regia", so called because it is the place where the Pope used to receive there the kings or their ambassadors.

The "Pauline Chapel" is named after Pope Paul III who, around 1540, commissioned the architect Antonio Sangallo the Younger to build it. It has two imposing frescoes by Michelangelo: "The Conversion of St. Paul" and "The Crucifixion of St. Peter".

On the first day of the conclave, the cardinals gather in the Pauline Chapel before solemnly entering the Sistine Chapel. Also there, the cardinal electors concelebrate the solemn Mass "De Spiritu Sancto" every day of the conclave to invoke God's help.

282. Cfr. Ordo Rituum Conclavis, Year 2000, n. 33.
283. Cfr. Apostolic Constitution Universi Dominici Gregis (February 22, 1996) n. 50.

What do they pray aloud as they make their way to the Sistine Chapel?

The cardinals sing the Litany of the Saints, in which they ask for the help of great figures of Christianity, both from the East and the West. They are saints who represent all the countries of the earth, including for example the martyrs of Canada, Uganda, Oceania, or Korea[284].

What do cardinal electors do when they enter the Sistine Chapel?

The first thing they do once they have all entered is to invoke the help of the Holy Spirit by singing the "Veni Creator" ("Come Creator Spirit"), a hymn in Latin that solemnly requests his presence and aid.

It is a monophonic melody sung "a capella" and in unison, generally by male voices, without instrumental accompaniment. The same music is repeated in each stanza with different lyrics. The text of the "Veni Creator" dates to the 9th century and is usually attributed to Rábano Mauro, a German Benedictine monk, writer, philosopher and theologian.

When they finish the chant they proceed with the oath.

284. Cfr. "Sede Apostolica Vacante. Storia - Legislazione - Riti - Luoghi e cose". Ufficio delle Celebrazioni Liturgiche del Sommo Pontefice. Vatican City, 2005.

What are the Latin lyrics of the hymn "Veni Creator"?

Veni Creator Spiritus,
Mentes tuorum visita,
Imple superna gratia,
Quae tu creasti, pectora.

Qui diceris Paraclitus,
Altissimi donum Dei,
Fons vivus, ignis, caritas,
Et spiritalis unctio.

Tu septiformis munere,
Digitus Paternae dexterae,
Tu rite promissum Patris,
Sermone ditans guttura.

Accende lumen sensibus,
Infunde amorem cordibus,
Infirma nostri corporis,
Virtute firmans perpeti.

Hostem repellas longius,
Pacemque dones protinus;
Ductore sic te praevio,
Vitemus omne noxium.

Per te sciamus da Patrem
Noscamus atque Filium;
Teque utriusque Spiritum
Credamus omni tempore.

Deo Patri sit gloria,
Et Filio, qui a mortuis
Surrexit, ac Paraclito
In saeculorum saecula.
Amen.

What is the translation of the hymn "Veni Creator"?

Come, Holy Spirit, Creator come,
From your bright heavenly throne!
Come, take possession of our souls,
And make them all your own.

You who are called the Paraclete,
Best gift of God above,
The living spring, the living fire,
Sweet unction, and true love!

You who are sevenfold in your grace,
Finger of God's right hand,
His promise, teaching little ones
To speak and understand!

O guide our minds with your blessed light,
With love our hearts inflame,
And with your strength which never decays
Confirm our mortal frame.

Far from us drive our hellish foe
True peace unto us bring,
And through all perils guide us safe
Beneath your sacred wing.

Through you may we the Father know,
Through you the eternal Son
And you the Spirit of them both
Thrice-blessed three in one.

All glory to the Father be,
And to the risen Son;
The same to you, O Paraclete,
While endless ages run. Amen.

How does the Holy Spirit act in the conclave?

The Holy Spirit "assists" the cardinals in the election of the new pontiff. Cardinal Joseph Ratzinger explained in 1997 in an interview to a Bavarian television station that this does not mean that God "dictates" the name of the candidate, but that he "acts as a teacher." "I would not say that the Holy Spirit chooses the pope, because it is not that he takes control of the situation, but that he acts as a good teacher, who leaves a lot of space, a lot of freedom, without abandoning us," he explained. In fact, "there are many popes that the Holy Spirit probably would not have chosen," he stressed at the time. "The role of the Holy Spirit must be understood in a more flexible way. It is not that he dictates the candidate to vote for. Probably the only guarantee he offers is that we don't totally screw things up," he clarified.

What is the oath that cardinals take in the Sistine Chapel?

It is a commitment to observe the rules of the conclave; that whoever is elected will fulfill the mission entrusted by Jesus to the apostle Peter; that he will observe the secrecy of what happens in the conclave; that he will not support or facilitate outside interference.

The cardinal dean, or if he is over 80 years of age, the oldest according to the order of precedence, reads the oath aloud, and then each of the cardinal electors, with one hand on the Gospels, renews the oath[285].

Then, each of them occupies the seat that corre-

285. Cfr. Apostolic Constitution Universi Dominici Gregis (February 22, 1996) n. 52.

sponds to him, following the order of precedence. Those closest to the altar are the cardinals of the order of bishops, then those of the order of priests, and then those of the order of deacons.

What is the formula of the oath that they take in the Sistine Chapel, immediately before beginning the election process?

It is this formula:

"We, the Cardinal electors present in this election of the Supreme Pontiff promise, pledge and swear, as individuals and as a group, to observe faithfully and scrupulously the prescriptions contained in the Apostolic Constitution of the Supreme Pontiff John Paul II, Universi Dominici Gregis, published on 22 February 1996.

We likewise promise, pledge and swear that whichever of us by divine disposition is elected Roman Pontiff will commit himself faithfully to carrying out the munus Petrinum of Pastor of the Universal Church and will not fail to affirm and defend strenuously the spiritual and temporal rights and the liberty of the Holy See.

In a particular way, we promise and swear to observe with the greatest fidelity and with all persons, clerical or lay, secrecy regarding everything that in any way relates to the election of the Roman Pontiff and regarding what occurs in the place of the election, directly or indirectly related to the results of the voting; we promise and swear not to break this secret in any way, either during or after the election of the new Pontiff, unless explicit authorization is granted by the same Pontiff; and never to lend support or favour to any interference, opposition or any other form of intervention, whereby secular authorities of whatever order and degree or any group of people or individuals might wish to intervene in the election of the Roman Pontiff"[286].

Next, the cardinal electors line up in order of precedence and approach a volume of the Gospels resting on a lectern. There, he will rest one hand on the book and take the oath with the following formula:

"And I, N. Cardinal N., do so promise, pledge and swear".

And laying his hand on the Gospels, he will add:

"So help me God and these Holy Gospels which I touch with my hand"[287].

From that moment on, they are ready to start voting.

286. Cfr. Apostolic Constitution Universi Dominici Gregis (February 22, 1996) n. 53.
287. Ibid.

Extra omnes!

Who can witness the voting of the cardinal electors?

Only the cardinal electors may be present, with no witnesses other than themselves. For this reason, before voting begins, the Master of Papal Liturgical Celebrations pronounces the "Extra omnes!", or "All out" to invite those who cannot be there to leave the Sistine Chapel.

Who pronounces the "Extra omnes!"?

It is pronounced by the Master of Liturgical Ceremonies. He does so once all the cardinals have taken the oath.

Who are the people responsible for watching out for spies in the Sistine Chapel?

Rather than "spies," the key is to prevent "possible threats to the independence of judgment and freedom of decision" of the cardinal electors[288]. For this reason, "the Cardinal Camerlengo and the three

288. Cfr. Apostolic Constitution Universi Dominici Gregis (February 22, 1996) n. 61.

Cardinal Assistants pro tempore are obliged to be especially vigilant in ensuring that there is absolutely no violation of secrecy with regard to the events occurring in the Sistine Chapel, where the voting takes place, and in the adjacent areas, before, as well as during and after the voting"[289].

To achieve this, they are allowed to make use of "the expertise of two trustworthy technicians" who "shall make every effort to preserve that secrecy by ensuring that no audiovisual equipment for recording or transmitting has been installed by anyone"[290].

What is the penalty for anyone who tries to spy on the deliberations in the Sistine Chapel?

The norm on the conclave prepared by John Paul II details that "should any infraction whatsoever of this norm occur and be discovered, those responsible should know that they will be subject to grave penalties according to the judgment of the future Pope"[291].

What happens if any of the people who have been admitted to provide technical or medical services broadcast to the outside world what happens?

If they "directly or indirectly" violate the secrecy, for example "by words or writing, by signs or in any other way," they would incur the penalty of excommunication latae sententiae (automatic) reserved to the Apostolic See"[292], that only the new pope could lift.

289. Cfr. Apostolic Constitution Universi Dominici Gregis (February 22, 1996) n. 55.
290. Ibid.
291. Ibid.

At what point do those who are not cardinal electors leave the Sistine Chapel?

Immediately "when the last of the Cardinal electors has taken the oath, the Master of Papal Liturgical Celebrations will give the order Extra omnes, and all those not taking part in the Conclave must leave the Sistine Chapel".

At that time, apart from the cardinal electors, only the Master of the Pontifical Liturgical Celebrations and the ecclesiastic to whom the "General Congregation" has entrusted a meditation "concerning the grave duty incumbent on them and thus on the need to act with right intention for the good of the Universal Church, solum Deum prae oculis habentes"[293] ("having only the will of God as a reference") may remain inside the Sistine Chapel. The preacher is usually a cardinal over 80 years of age, who cannot vote.

After the meditation, both the preacher and the Master of Papal Liturgical Celebrations will leave the chapel and leave the cardinals alone to vote.

What will be the theme of the preaching that the cardinals will hear before they begin to vote?

The meditation will concern "the grave duty incumbent on them and thus on the need to act with right intention for the good of the Universal Church, solum Deum prae oculis habentes"[294], that is, "having only the will of God as a reference".

292. Cfr. Apostolic Constitution Universi Dominici Gregis (February 22, 1996) n. 58.
293. Cfr. Apostolic Constitution Universi Dominici Gregis (February 22, 1996) n. 52.
294. Cfr. Apostolic Constitution Universi Dominici Gregis (February 22, 1996) n. 52.

Do the preacher and the Master of the Celebrations remain in the Sistine Chapel during the voting?

No. After the meditation, both "leave the Sistine Chapel, the doors are closed and guards are posted at all the chapel entrances"[295].

Who should close the door of the Sistine Chapel once the non-voters have left?

The door will be closed by the last of the cardinal electors of the order of deacons, who will also be seated closest to the exit. This cardinal should open and close the door as many times as necessary during the conclave[296].

Who guards the doors of the Sistine Chapel?

Outside each of the entrances to the chapel there are two Swiss guards who prevent anyone from entering during the election[297].

Do you immediately begin voting once the cardinal electors have been left alone?

No. Once the Master of the Celebrations and the preacher have left, the cardinals recite a few prayers and the one presiding over the conclave - the cardinal dean or his substitute - asks the electors " whether the election can begin, or whether there still re-

295. Ordo Rituum Conclavis, Year 2000, n. 44.
296. Cfr. Apostolic Constitution Universi Dominici Gregis (February 22, 1996) n. 65.
297. Ordo Rituum Conclavis, Year 2000, n. 44.

main doubts which need to be clarified concerning the norms and procedures laid down" in the law of the conclave, the "Universi Dominici Gregis"[298]. It is the moment to resolve doubts, but not to change the rules. "It is not however permitted, even if the electors are unanimously agreed, to modify or replace any of the norms and procedures which are a substantial part of the election process, under penalty of the nullity of the same deliberation"[299].

If the majority of the electors agree to proceed with the election operations, the process of conducting the first scrutiny begins immediately[300].

What should Catholics do while the cardinals are meeting in the conclave?

The law asks Catholics to be united with their bishops "and especially with the cardinal electors" and to pray for the election[301]. "Thus, the election of the new Pope will not be something unconnected with the People of God and concerning the College of electors alone, but will be in a certain sense an act of the whole Church"[302]. They should pray to God "that he may enlighten the electors and make them so likeminded in their task that a speedy, harmonious and fruitful election may take place, as the salvation of souls and the good of the whole People of God demand"[303].

298. Cfr. Apostolic Constitution Universi Dominici Gregis (February 22, 1996) n. 54.
299. Ibid.
300. Ibid.
301. Cfr. Apostolic Constitution Universi Dominici Gregis (February 22, 1996) n. 84.
302. Ibid.
303. Ibid.

First scrutiny

Why is the first scrutiny important?

Because it is the moment of truth. In the first vote it will become clear who are the cardinals with the most support and who have a serious chance of becoming the next pope.

How many votes are required to be elected pope?

This is a fundamental rule of the conclave. The norm promulgated by John Paul II establishes that " for the valid election of the Roman Pontiff at least two thirds of the votes are required, calculated on the basis of the total number of electors present and voting"[304]. And "should it be impossible to divide the number of Cardinals present into three equal parts, for the validity of the election of the Supreme Pontiff one additional vote is required"[305], that is, two thirds plus one.

The conclave of March 2013 was attended by 115 cardinals. To be elected pope, two-thirds of the votes plus one, or 77 votes, were required.

304. Cfr. Apostolic Constitution Universi Dominici Gregis (February 22, 1996) n. 62.
305. Ibid.

How many voting sessions can there be each day?

On the first day, there will be at most one vote in the afternoon. On the following days there are two votes in the morning and two in the afternoon, at the time previously agreed upon by the General Congregations or in the assemblies of cardinal electors during the period of the election[306].

How many phases are there in each vote?

In every vote there are three phases called pre-scrutiny, scrutiny and post-scrutiny[307].

What does the pre-scrutiny phase consist of?

This first part is in turn developed in three steps.

First, the last of the cardinal deacons opens the door of the Sistine Chapel and ushers in the eight "ceremonieri" o Masters of Ceremonies. They distribute the ballots to the cardinals, give two or three to each elector in the Sistine Chapel, and take them to the sick cardinal electors who are in their rooms.

Then, a roll call of the cardinal electors present is taken and a small wooden ball with the name of each cardinal elector present in the Sistine Chapel is placed in a cloth bag to decide by lot who will be the scrutineers, revisers and "infirmarii" (the ones charged with collecting the votes of the sick)[308].

306. Cfr. Apostolic Constitution Universi Dominici Gregis (February 22, 1996) n. 63.
307. Cfr. Apostolic Constitution Universi Dominici Gregis (February 22, 1996) n. 64.
308. Cfr. "Sede Apostolica Vacante. Storia - Legislazione - Riti - Luoghi e cose". Ufficio delle Celebrazioni Liturgiche del Sommo Pontefice. Città del Vaticano, 2005. "Pre-scrutinio".

To draw the lots, the "ceremonieri" must have left the Sistine Chapel. The Master of Papal Liturgical Celebrations then announces the drawing of lots: "Nunc eligendi sunt Cardinales Scrutatores, Infirmarii et Recognitores", and the last of the cardinals of the order of deacons draws from the bag nine small balls on which the name of each elected cardinal will appear.

The first three are "scrutineers," who read the ballots; the second three are "infirmarii," who collect the votes of the convalescents; and the last three are "revisers," who verify the result of the vote. If among these nine elected there is a cardinal impeded by illness or other reason, more names may be drawn until cardinals are elected who can perform this function[309]. They will have this function during a single "voting session", either the morning or the afternoon one.

The positions will be drawn again at the beginning of the next session.

Who hands out the ballots?

This is done by eight "ceremonieri", who hand out two or three ballots to each cardinal elector in the Sistine Chapel and to the sick who are in the places adapted for them. Once distributed, they leave the Sistine Chapel[310].

309. Ibid.
310. Ordo Rituum Conclavis, Year 2000, n. 50.

How are the positions drawn?

The names of the cardinals are written on wooden balls placed inside a cloth bag. The last of the cardinal deacons draws nine balls at random and reads the names of those chosen. The first three will be the "scrutineers", the second three will be the "infirmarii" and the third three will be the "revisers". If a cardinal is drawn who, because of his condition, is unable to fulfill the assignment, a new name is drawn to fill his vacancy[311].

Can the Master of Papal Liturgical Celebrations and his assistants stay in the Sistine Chapel to assist in these operations?

Yes, but they must leave immediately before the cardinals begin to fill out the ballots. "During the voting, the cardinal electors must remain in the Sistine Chapel alone and therefore, immediately after the distribution of the ballots and before the electors begin to write, the Secretary of the College of Cardinals, the Master of the Pontifical Liturgical Celebrations and the Ceremonieri must leave." The protocol states that "before the electors begin to write on the ballots, the Secretary of the College of Cardinals the Master of the Pontifical Liturgical Ceremonies and the Ceremonieri must leave the room"[312].

311. Cfr. "Sede Apostolica Vacante. Storia - Legislazione - Riti - Luoghi e cose". Ufficio delle Celebrazioni Liturgiche del Sommo Pontefice. Vatican City, 2005.
312. Ordo Rituum Conclavis, Year 2000, n. 51.

Who can open or close the door of the Sistine Chapel?

The person in charge of opening or closing the door when necessary is the last cardinal deacon[313]. He opens and closes the door with a key from the inside and takes the key back to its place.

How many ballot boxes are used in the conclave?

Three are used: one for voting, one to collect the votes of sick cardinal electors who cannot enter the Sistine Chapel, and a third to collect the ballots after the scrutiny and take them to the stoves where they will be burned[314]. While the ballot box is on the altar of the Sistine Chapel, the scrutiny takes place at a table in front of the altar.

What is the mission of the Cardinal Scrutineers?

They are responsible for guarding the ballot box, counting the votes to verify that they do not exceed the number of voters, and reading aloud the name written on the ballots.

What does the true and proper scrutiny phase consist of?

It includes the insertion of the ballots in the appropriate ballot box; the mixing and counting of the ballots; and the counting of the votes[315].

313. Cfr. "Sede Apostolica Vacante. Storia - Legislazione - Riti - Luoghi e cose". Ufficio delle Celebrazioni Liturgiche del Sommo Pontefice. Vatican City, 2005.
314. Ordo Rituum Conclavis, Year 2000, n. 51.
315. Cfr. Apostolic Constitution Universi Dominici Gregis (February 22, 1996) n. 66.

What characteristics should the ballots for the papal election have?

The law of the conclave even establishes how the ballots should be. "The ballot must be rectangular in shape and have written on the upper half, if possible printed, the words: 'Eligo in Summum Pontificem', ("I choose Supreme Pontiff"), while on the lower half space must be left to write the name of the elected; the ballot is therefore made in such a way that it can be folded in half"[316].

How to fill in the ballot?

The law states that it must be filled out "in secret by each cardinal voter"[317]. The idea is that he will write a single name, with a handwriting that prevents the voter's identity from being recognized. Then, he will fold it twice[318].

Is it possible to identify the handwriting of the person who wrote the name on the ballot?

The law of the conclave recommends that cardinal electors write the name of their candidate using a different handwriting than usual and as unrecognizable as possible[319].

What happens if two names are written on the ballot?

If two candidates' names are written on the ballot,

316. Cfr. Apostolic Constitution Universi Dominici Gregis (February 22, 1996) n. 65.
317. Ibid.
318. Ibid.
319. Ibid.

that vote is declared invalid[320].

Can you write the name of someone who is not a cardinal?

Yes, they can vote for any person who meets the conditions to be appointed bishop of Rome. It is said that in the 1958 conclave Giovanni Battista Montini, then archbishop of Milan, but not a cardinal, received some votes. He was elected pope five years later, in 1963.

In what form is the ballot folded?

After writing down the name, the voter must fold the ballot twice to prevent the name he has written from being seen[321].

Should the cardinals be alone while writing the name of the chosen one?

Yes, in fact, immediately after the distribution of the ballots and before the electors begin to write, the Secretary of the College of Cardinals, the Master of the Pontifical Liturgical Celebrations and the eight Ceremonieri must leave the Sistine Chapel. They are accompanied to the exit by the last of the Cardinals of the Order of Deacons, who is in charge of closing and opening the door[322].

320. Ibid.
321. Ibid.
322. Ibid.

How do they vote?

To vote, once the name has been written on the ballot, and after having folded it twice, the cardinals line up in order of precedence to go to the ballot box, which is on the altar of the Sistine Chapel. With the ballot in his hand, he "holds it up so that it can be seen and carries it to the altar, at which the Scrutineers stand and upon which there is placed a receptacle, covered by a plate, for receiving the ballots"[323].

Before casting the vote, each cardinal must pronounce aloud this oath: "I call as my witness Christ the Lord who will be my judge, that my vote is given to the one who before God I think should be elected".

Then, he deposits the vote, bows before the altar and returns to the place where he has his seat.

The three scrutineers wait on both sides of the altar, next to the ballot boxes, and vote when it is their turn according to precedence.

Where should the ballot box be?

The ballot box will be in the Sistine Chapel, on the altar beneath the frescoes of the Last Judgment[324].

What does the ballot box look like?

In the past, a chalice and ciborium were used to collect the votes. John Paul II established that a specific ballot box should be prepared.

323. Cfr. Apostolic Constitution Universi Dominici Gregis (February 22, 1996) n. 66.
324. Ibid.

The current one used to vote is oval in shape, made of silver and bronze. It has a plate on top in which the ballot is placed to introduce it through the slot. It is decorated with motifs relating to Jesus as the Good Shepherd, and Eucharistic symbols such as grapes and ears of wheat.

There are two other ballot boxes: one locked to collect the votes of sick cardinals, and the other to collect the ballots during the count and then burn them. They were made by the Italian sculptor Cecco Bonanotte, who also designed the entrance doors to the Vatican Museums inaugurated in 2000.

Who should be in front of the ballot box?

The three cardinal scrutineers, as those responsible for guarding the ballot boxes.

Who inserts the ballots in the ballot box?

Each voter folds the ballot, approaches the altar holding it visibly in his hand. Having arrived before the ballot box, he pronounces an oath, rests the ballot on the plate, and with the help of it he personally introduces it through the opening of the ballot box[325].

In what order do the cardinals approach the ballot box?

In order of precedence, according to the hierarchy

325. Ibid.

of the three orders (bishops, presbyters and deacons) and seniority.

Is the vote placed directly into the ballot box?

No. Each cardinal first places it on the plate that covers the opening of the ballot box, and then inserts it into the box[326].

Is the vote done silently?

No. Before casting the vote, each cardinal must pronounce aloud the following formula of oath:

"I call as my witness Christ the Lord who will be my judge, that my vote is given to the one who before God I think should be elected".

When he has done this, he places the ballot on the plate, inserts it through the opening, bows before the altar and returns to his place[327].

Who casts the vote of the sick cardinals present in the Sistine Chapel who are unable to approach the ballot box?

If they are in the Sistine Chapel but cannot move to the ballot box, the last of the three cardinal scrutineers approaches them. The sick cardinal then pronounces the aforementioned oath and hands the scrutinizer the folded ballot, which the scrutinizer carries visibly to the altar. There, he places it on the

326 Ibid.
327. Ibid.

plate and inserts it into the ballot box[328].

How are the votes of sick Cardinal electors who are not in the Sistine Chapel collected?

The three cardinals "infirmarii" collect the votes of the sick cardinals who are participating in the conclave but cannot go to the Sistine Chapel. The "infirmarii" will be able to "complete their own ballots and place them in the receptable immediately after the senior Cardinal, and then go to collect the votes of the sick"[329] and thus not make the wait too long.

The scrutineers give them a locked ballot box where they can collect the votes of the sick. Before they leave the Sistine Chapel, they open it, show that there is no ballot inside, lock it, and leave the key on the altar. The three "infirmarii" then go to the room of each convalescing cardinal in Casa Santa Marta, and bring a sufficient number of ballots and the locked ballot box. This has an opening through which the sick cardinal can insert the folded ballot.

When they return to the Sistine Chapel, this urn is opened and it is verified that the number of votes corresponds to the number of sick cardinals. Then, they put them one by one on the plate and with this they put them all together in the ballot box[330].

328 Ibid.
329. Cfr. Apostolic Constitution Universi Dominici Gregis (February 22, 1996) n. 67.
330. Ibid.

How do you check that the ballot box for the "infirmarii" is empty?

Before the cardinal scrutineers hand the box to the three cardinal "infirmarii", they must open it in front of the rest of the electors, so that the cardinals can verify that it is empty. They then close it, place the key on the altar and hand it to them to collect the votes of the convalescents[331].

How do sick voters vote at Casa Santa Marta?

They must vote in secret, without anyone seeing them. Like the rest of the electors, they write the name of the chosen one on the ballot paper, fold it, pronounce the oath, and introduce it through the opening into the ballot box carried by the cardinal "infirmarii"[332].

What happens if a sick constituent is unable to write?

In that case, it will be written on his behalf by one of the three cardinal "infirmarii" or another cardinal elector chosen by the sick person, after having sworn before the "infirmarii" that he will maintain the secrecy of the name he has chosen[333].

331 Ibid.
332. Ibid.
333. Ibid.

Counting and election

What is done in the part of the election known as post-scrutiny?

In this part, the votes are counted, the cardinal revisers oversee the result and if necessary, the ballots are burned in the same place where the voting took place[334].

How are votes counted?

It is performed by the three "cardinal scrutineers", who must be seated at "a table placed in front of the altar"[335]. It is a table covered with a cloth, and with six chairs. There are two chairs on the side facing the altar, which are for the first two scrutineers. Another chair is placed on the left side. The other three chairs, with their backs to the nave, are for the three cardinals who will sit before the scrutineers once the count is concluded, to recount the ballots one by one regardless of the result[336].

334. Cfr. Apostolic Constitution Universi Dominici Gregis (February 22, 1996) n. 70.
335. Cfr. Apostolic Constitution Universi Dominici Gregis (February 22, 1996) n. 68
336. Cfr. "Sede Apostolica Vacante. Storia - Legislazione - Riti - Luoghi e cose". Ufficio delle Celebrazioni Liturgiche del Sommo Pontefice. Vatican City, 2005.

After all the voters have placed their ballot in the ballot box, the first scrutineer "shakes it several times in order to mix them"[337]. The third scrutineer then counts them "picking them out of the urn in full view and placing them in another empty receptacle previously prepared for this purpose"[338].

"If the number of ballots does not correspond to the number of electors, the ballots must all be burned and a second vote taken at once," without opening any of the ballots[339]. This is what happened in the fifth scrutiny of the March 2013 conclave, when a cardinal mistakenly inserted two ballots instead of one, and the vote had to be repeated. "If however their number does correspond to the number of electors, the opening of the ballots then takes place"[340].

What happens if the number of ballots is more or less than the number of electors?

"If the number of ballots does not correspond to the number of electors, the ballots must all be burned and a second vote taken at once"[341]. That is to say, a new vote is taken immediately without opening any ballot paper. It happened for example in the fifth scrutiny of the March conclave of 2013, when a cardinal mistakenly inserted two ballots instead of one. The ballots of the annulled scrutiny are burned together with those of the successive ballot, which is the correct one; and therefore, with them there is no fumata.

337. Cfr. Apostolic Constitution Universi Dominici Gregis (February 22, 1996) n. 68.
338. Ibid.
339. Ibid.
340. Ibid.
341. Ibid.

What happens if at the time of counting, when unfolding them, a double ballot appears?

"If during the opening of the ballots the Scrutineers should discover two ballots folded in such a way that they appear to have been completed by one elector, if these ballots bear the same name they are counted as one vote; if however they bear two different names, neither vote will be valid; however, in neither of the two cases is the voting session annulled"[342].

What happens if the ballot is blank?

If the ballot is blank, the vote does not go to any candidate, but it counts for the two-thirds count.

How is the count done?

If the number of cardinals voting and the number of ballots coincide, the recount begins.

The three scrutineers are seated at a table before the altar of the Sistine Chapel. The first of them takes a ballot, opens it, reads the name that appears and passes it to the second scrutineer who reads the name and passes it to the third. The latter reads the name aloud and intelligibly so that all present can write down the vote on a sheet of paper. This third scrutineer must also write down the name on each ballot paper[343]. In addition, "as he reads out the individual ballots, pierces each one with a needle through the word Eligo and places it on a thread, so that the ballots can be more securely preserved". This makes it

342. Cfr. Apostolic Constitution Universi Dominici Gregis (February 22, 1996) n. 69.
343. Cfr. Apostolic Constitution Universi Dominici Gregis (February 22, 1996) n. 69.

possible to check that they have already been counted[344].

When the scrutiny is concluded, the three cardinals add up the votes obtained by each cardinal and write them on a sheet of paper. They also tie the ends of the thread that has been inserted into the ballots, and leave them in a container or at the side of the table.

If someone has obtained a two-thirds majority, or two-thirds plus one in case the fraction is not exact, the election of the new pope is canonically valid[345]. He is not yet pope, for it is necessary for him to accept the election.

No matter the case, whether or not the necessary majority was obtained, the three "cardinal revisers" approach the table to review and recount all the votes. "The Revisers must proceed to check both the ballots and the notes made by the Scrutineers, in order to make sure that these latter have performed their task exactly and faithfully"[346].

What is done after reading the ballots?

Once the ballots have been read, the scrutineers add up the votes obtained by each cardinal and write them down on a separate sheet of paper. In addition, the third cardinal scrutineer ties a knot in the thread with which he has sewn the ballots, so that no more ballots can be inserted.

344. Ibid.
345. Cfr. Apostolic Constitution Universi Dominici Gregis (February 22, 1996) n. 70.
346. Ibid.

When are the ballots burned?

Ballots are burned only once in the morning and once in the afternoon. Two ballots are scheduled in the morning and two in the afternoon. "If however a second vote is to take place immediately, the ballots from the first vote will be burned only at the end, together with those from the second vote"[347]. The ballots are burned "before the Cardinal electors leave the Sistine Chapel"[348].

Who is responsible for burning the conclave ballots?

They are to be burned in the stove prepared in the Sistine Chapel "by the Scrutineers, with the assistance of the Secretary of the Conclave and the Masters of Ceremonies," called by the last cardinal deacon once the count has been completed and verified"[349].

They will add fumigants to the smoke. The color black is used to communicate that no cardinal has obtained the necessary majority, and white, that he has now been elected.

To preserve secrecy more securely, the writings of any kind that the cardinals have taken with them should also be burned[350].

How are the ballots burned?

The ballots are burned in a stove that is set up during the conclave inside the Sistine Chapel. Its chim-

347. Ibid.
348. Ibid.
349. Ibid.
350. Cfr. Ordo Rituum Conclavis, Year 2000, n.56

ney exits through the roof of the chapel and the color of the smoke acts as a signal to the outside world that the conclave must continue or that a new pope has been elected.

When was the stove in which the ballots are currently burned first used?

The current stove with which the ballots are burned was used for the first time in the conclave of March 1939, when Eugenio Pacelli, Pius XII, was elected pope. Engraved on its lid are the years and months of the conclaves in which it has been used: 1939/III, which is when Pius XII was elected; 1958/X, which was the election of John XXIII; 1963/VI, that of Paul VI; 1978/VIII, the election of John Paul I; 1978/X, the election of John Paul II; 2005/IV, that of Benedict XVI; and 2013/III, that of Pope Francis.

However, since 2005, another auxiliary stove, connected to the same chimney, has also been used. Fumigants are introduced into this stove to give a clear color to the smoke so that there is no doubt as to whether it is black or white.

Is the stove permanent in the Sistine Chapel?

No. It is carefully kept by the staff of the pontifical ceremonies and is installed only during the conclave.

What are the characteristics of the stove?

The stove where the ballots are burned is cylindrical, made of iron, dark gray in color, and measures only one meter in height and 45 centimeters in diameter. It has a lower door where the fire is lit, with a manual draft control valve.

The ballots and notes are inserted through an upper opening and burned every two ballots (after the last one in the morning and the last one in the afternoon). On that opening are engraved the years and months of the conclaves in which it has been used: 1939/III, which is when Pius XII was elected; 1958/X, which was the election of John XXIII; 1963/VI, that of Paul VI; 1978/VIII, the election of John Paul I; 1978/X, election of John Paul II; 2005/IV, that of Benedict XVI; and 2013/III, that of Pope Francis.

There is a second stove that is used to introduce black or white fumigants into the chimney, so that they give a clear color to the smoke and there is no doubt as to whether it is black or white. The two stoves share a chimney that exits through the roof of the Sistine Chapel.

The outside of the chimney is almost two meters high so that it is visible from the whole of St. Peter's Square. To facilitate the circulation of smoke, the chimney is heated by electric heaters and has a fan that comes into operation if necessary.

What is the fumata?

"Fumata" is an Italian word meaning "smoke". It is the traditional procedure to inform the pilgrims about the result of the voting, without giving them the name of the elected. After voting, the ballots are burned in a stove located inside the Sistine Chapel and fumigants are added. From there, smoke exits a chimney extending from the roof overlooking St. Peter's Square. The "fumata" it produces can be white or black. If it is black, it means that no candidate has obtained a sufficient majority. If it is white, it means that the Catholic Church has a new pope.

Since when has smoke been used to communicate the outcome of a conclave?

In 1823, during the conclave, the Romans were attentive to the smoke coming out of the chimney of the Quirinal, as it was the agreed signal for the guard corps to fire blanks and announce to all of Rome that a new pope had been elected[351]. The first time that white smoke was used to communicate the election to the people was in the conclave of 1914.

Are any other elements added to the "fumata" to color the smoke?

Yes, since 1958 products have been used to color the smoke. During the election of Benedict XVI, in April 2005, an auxiliary stove was used for the first time which, thanks to an electronic mechanism and chemical products, made it possible to increase the visibility of the smoke.

351. Cfr. "Sede Apostolica Vacante. Storia - Legislazione - Riti - Luoghi e cose". Ufficio delle Celebrazioni Liturgiche del Sommo Pontefice. Vatican City, 2005.

Are any other documents burned along with the ballots?

"In order that secrecy may be better observed," John Paul II "ordered" the cardinal electors to "hand over to the Cardinal Camerlengo or to one of the three Cardinal Assistants any notes which he may have in his possession concerning the results of each ballot", and that "these notes are to be burnt together with the ballots"[352].

At what times are the "fumata"?

Due to the schedule of the conclave, the morning and afternoon ballots end at around 12:00 and 19:00. If elected in the first ballot, the white smoke could be brought forward one hour.

What happens if no cardinal is elected pope after the first vote in the morning or afternoon?

In that case, they vote again, without having to take the oath again or elect new cardinal scrutineers, infirmarii or revisers. In this second scrutiny, the drawing of lots in the first scrutiny is valid, without repeating anything[353].

352. Cfr. Apostolic Constitution Universi Dominici Gregis (February 22, 1996) n. 71.
353. Cfr. Apostolic Constitution Universi Dominici Gregis (February 22, 1996) n. 72.

Should the cardinals do anything else before leaving the Sistine Chapel?

"Each election session closes with a brief act of thanksgiving and an invocation to the Blessed Virgin Mary"[354].

How long do the cardinals have to elect a new pope?

There are no deadlines. However, if after three days of voting (12-13 ballots) no one has been elected, "voting is to be suspended for a maximum of one day in order to allow a pause for prayer, informal discussion among the voters, and a brief spiritual exhortation given by the senior Cardinal in the Order of Deacons".

If after seven more scrutinies (a total of 19-20 ballots) there is still no new pope, "another pause for prayer, discussion" and an exhortation is given by the senior Cardinal in the Order of Priests. Then, they will vote again.

If after seven more scrutinies (cumulative total, 26-27 ballots) a positive result is not reached, another "pause for prayer, discussion and an exhortation given by the senior Cardinal in the Order of Bishops", on the delicacy of the moment they are going through.

If after another seven ballots there is no result, Benedict XVI established that "one day shall be dedicated to prayer, reflection and dialogue" and that thereafter, in the successive ballots, they should choose only between the two candidates who in the last election

354. Cfr. Ordo Rituum Conclavis, Year 2000, n. 57.

had the most votes, and who will not be able to vote[355]. In order to be elected pope, no matter what, "for a valid election to take place there must be a clear majority of at least two thirds of the votes of the Cardinals present and voting"[356].

How many days off can they take if they cannot reach an agreement?

The answer is a bit complex, but this general outline assumes that the first vote is the same evening that the conclave begins.

If the thirteen ballots are reached without electing a Pope, the fifth day is a full day of rest and free conversation.

On the sixth day there are four scrutinies and on the seventh day, another three. If there is no Pope, at this point there have been 20 scrutinies, the pause is made on the evening of the seventh day, after the only vote.

On the eighth day there are again four scrutinies and on the ninth, three more. If there is no agreement, on the ninth day, after the voting of the afternoon, which is number 27, there is another pause for prayer, free conversation and the first cardinal of the order of bishops addresses a meditation to all the electors.

On day ten they vote again four times, twice in the morning and twice in the afternoon; and on day eleven, another three times. That would be a total of 34 scrutinies. At that point, the Sede Vacante has lasted

355. Motu Proprio "Normas Nonnullas", Benedict XVI, 22 February 2013. Art. 75.
356. Ibid.

between 26 and 31 days.

If the Pope has not been elected yet, on that day the voting is suspended for the fourth time and invited by the Camarlengo, they will have to decide by absolute majority whether to let a few days pass before voting again or to take other measures. The most important thing is that from that moment on, the 35th ballot - or the 34th if no vote was taken on the first evening - the candidates will be only the two most voted for in the last ballot and (if they are electors) neither of them would have the right to vote. To be elected pope, he would still need a majority of at least two-thirds "of the votes of the Cardinals present and voting".

For more than two centuries there has been no need for so many votes and scrutinies.

Can the cardinal with the most votes refuse the election?

Yes, he can. In the law of the conclave, John Paul II addresses him and tells him that, if the reason for the resignation is "for fear of its weight", it is better "to submit humbly to the design of the divine will"[357]. With a perspective of faith, he reminds him that "God who imposes the burden will sustain him with his hand, so that he will be able to bear it. In conferring the heavy task upon him, God will also help him to accomplish it and, in giving him the dignity, he will grant him the strength not to be overwhelmed by the weight of his office"[358]. However, if there is some serious reason that conditions him, it is better for him to refuse.

357. Cfr. Apostolic Constitution Universi Dominici Gregis (February 22, 1996) n. 86.
358. Ibid.

White smoke

What happens in the Sistine Chapel if a cardinal achieves at least two-thirds of the votes and is elected Pope?

Once the count has been reviewed and it has been confirmed that he has exceeded two-thirds of the votes, he must be asked if he accepts the election and he must give his explicit consent.

What happens if the elected person does not accept the position?

If he does not accept the office, the scrutinies are resumed until a new pope is elected.

What happens if the chosen one is not in the Sistine Chapel?

The law of the conclave refers to the "Ordo rituum Conclavis", the liturgical document that guides the celebration of the conclave[359]. It explains that "if the

359. The edition used to prepare this volume is the latest known edition of the "Ordo rituum Conclavis", updated in 2000.

elect resides outside Vatican City, appropriate norms must be given so that he may be conducted as soon as possible to the conclave"[360], and proposes that the electors elect "two cardinals who assist the presiding cardinal until the new pope arrives and accepts the election"[361].

With great discretion, these three cardinals "will call the substitute for the Secretary of State, who will cautiously see to it that the chosen one arrives in Rome as soon as possible, absolutely avoiding the media, so that the secrecy of the conclave is not violated"[362].

When the elect arrives in Vatican City, the substitute will inform the Cardinal President and carry out his orders exactly. Then, "after consulting with the two cardinals assisting him, he will summon the cardinal electors and introduce the one elected into the Sistine Chapel, so that the rite of acceptance may be celebrated"[363].

How is the elected official asked if he accepts the position?

First, the last of the Cardinal Deacons opens the door of the Sistine Chapel and requests that the Secretary of the College of Cardinals, the Master of the Pontifical Liturgical Celebrations and two Ceremonieri enter.

With them as witnesses, the Cardinal Dean, or if he is the one elected or impeded, the Vice-Dean, or in his place, the first of the Cardinals in order and sen-

360. Cfr. "Ordo rituum Conclavis", Year 2000, n. 10.
361. Cfr. "Ordo rituum Conclavis", Year 2000, n. 62.
362. Ibid.
363. Ibid.

iority, in the name of the whole college of electors, approaches the one who has been elected and asks him a direct question:

"*Acceptasne electionem de te canonice factam in Summum Pontificem?*", "Do you accept your canonical election as Supreme Pontiff?". If he answers yes and is already a bishop, he automatically becomes pope.

Then the same cardinal asks him a second fundamental question: "*Quo nomine vis vocari*", that is, "By what name do you wish to be called?". The new pope can answer in Latin or as he prefers, but this formula is proposed: "*Vocabor (name)*". "I will be called..."

After hearing the response, "the Master of Papal Liturgical Celebrations, acting as notary and having as witnesses the two Masters of Ceremonies, draws up a document certifying acceptance by the new Pope and the name taken by him"[364].

What answers can the chosen one give when asked if he accepts?

You can respond in three ways: affirmatively, negatively or remain silent.

The negative answer would be "*Non accepto*" or "*Non accipio*". He can also remain silent, in which case the cardinal electors will have to consider what time limit to give him until he gives a definitive answer.

364. Cfr. Apostolic Constitution Universi Dominici Gregis (February 22, 1996) n. 87.

Is the rite of lowering the canopy still used in the Papal election?

No. In the past, each of the cardinal electors sat in the Sistine Chapel under a small canopy. When one of them accepted to become pope, the others would lower their canopy as a gesture of respect, so that only the one of the elected remained open. It was a way of recognizing and honoring the new pontiff.

The last time it was used was in 1963, on the occasion of the election of Pope Paul VI. As the number of electors increased in the last conclaves, it was necessary to place several rows of chairs, and the canopy of the chairs in front of them hindered the visibility of those in the back. This situation meant that the canopies had to be eliminated and, therefore, the custom of lowering them.

At what point does the elect acquire full and supreme power over the Church?

If the elected cardinal is a bishop, immediately upon acceptance he becomes "Bishop of the Church of Rome, true Pope and Head of the College of Bishops. He thus acquires and can exercise full and supreme power over the universal Church"[365]. If he is not a bishop, he must be ordained, in a ceremony to be held there immediately, before announcing the election. Once ordained, he becomes pope.

365. Cfr. Apostolic Constitution Universi Dominici Gregis (February 22, 1996) n. 88.

Who ordains him bishop?

If the one elected is not a bishop, he will be ordained "by the Dean of the College of Cardinals or, in his absence, by the Subdean or, should he too be prevented from doing so, by the senior Cardinal Bishop"[366] in a ceremony to be held immediately after his acceptance.

When does the new pope wear white?

The law of the conclave does not state this, but refers to the "Ordo rituum Conclavis", the ritual of the conclave, which mentions that once he accepts the election and announces his name, "the Pontiff, after having vested himself in the Sacristy with the help of the Master of the Pontifical Liturgical Celebrations, returns to the Sistine Chapel and sits on the Chair"[367]. In the sacristy he must put on "the vestments proper to him", and therefore he leaves there dressed in white[368].

It is traditional that the secretary of the conclave gives him the white biretta. It is customary for the new pope in return to place on him his cardinal's biretta, as a way of announcing that he will make him prince of the Church in his first consistory. The new pope is not obliged to do so.

366. Cfr. Apostolic Constitution Universi Dominici Gregis (February 22, 1996) n. 90.
367. Cfr. Ordo Rituum Conclavis, Year 2000, n. 67.
368. Ibid.

Where is he seen for the first time wearing the white cassock?

In the sacristy of the Sistine Chapel. This place, according to tradition, is called the "Room of Tears" in commemoration of the shock that the chosen one supposedly experiences when he dresses in white for the first time. There, three white cassocks of three different sizes await him, so that he can wear the one that fits him best.

Is it true that there are three white cassocks for the new pope to wear the one that best suits him?

Yes, there are at least three white cassocks. It is impossible to foresee the size of the one who will be elected pope, and to have a perfect cassock ready for him. Therefore, the Master of Papal Liturgical Celebrations arranges for at least three to be ready, in small, medium and large sizes. He also has several pairs of shoes available. The chosen one is dressed in the cassock that best suits him and some quick alterations are made for his first presentation. On this occasion, the pontiffs usually wear a white cassock, a red capelet, a red stole and a white skullcap.

How does the world find out that a new pope has been elected?

The sign that a new pope has been elected is the white smoke rising from the chimney of the Sistine Chapel.

In the past, the ballots for each scrutiny were burned with wet straw to color the smoke black. If no straw was added, the smoke was white and meant that there was a new pontiff. The truth is that the color was not very clear and the result was not always clear. Nowadays, fumigants and chemical products are used to avoid doubts.

When are the ballots burned, and the "white smoke" announced?

They are burned after the acceptance, and while the Pope is changing in the sacristy of the Sistine Chapel. In addition to the ballots, the other writings kept by the cardinals are to be burned. The protocol adds that "it is appropriate that this time, with the advice of the technicians, white smoke, the so-called 'fumata bianca', should be released to the outside as a sign that the new Supreme Pontiff has been elected"[369].

Are there any other signs that a new pope has been elected?

Minutes after the white smoke, the six bells of St. Peter's Basilica will begin to toll.

What are the bells of St. Peter's Basilica called?

These are the "Campanone", cast in 1785, which weighs 8,950 kg, and has a diameter of 2.316 meters; the "Campanoncino", 1725, 3,640 kg, and 1.772 meters in diameter; the "Rota", of the thirteenth century, 1.815 kg and 1.361 m. in diameter; the "Prédica", 1909, 830 kg and 1.085 m. in diameter; the "Ave Ma-

369. Cfr. Ordo Rituum Conclavis, Year 2000, n. 66.

ria", 1932, 250 kg and 0.75 meters in diameter; and the "Campanella", 1825, 235 kg and a diameter of 0.73 meters. All are cast in bronze.

What is the first ceremony in which the newly elected pope participates?

If the one elected is already a bishop, which is the most usual, "after having been clothed in the sacristy with the help of the Master of the Pontifical Liturgical Celebrations with the vestments proper to him, he returns to the Sistine Chapel and is seated at the Chair"[370]. Then the dean, or whoever presides over the conclave, invites the new pope to listen to the Gospel passage with the words of Christ on the mission of the apostle Peter, whose successor he has just become.

The cardinal protodeacon (the first of the cardinals of the order of deacons) then reads the text from the gospel of Matthew 16:13-19[371]; or John 21:15-17[372]. After listening to these readings, the first of the cardinals of the order of presbyters pronounces a very brief prayer for the new pope. The cardinal electors then approach the pontiff following the order of precedence, to greet him personally and as an "act

370. Cfr. Ordo Rituum Conclavis, Year 2000, n. 67.
371. «When Jesus went into the region of Caesarea Philippi he asked his disciples, "Who do people say that the Son of Man is?" They replied, "Some say John the Baptist, others Elijah, still others Jeremiah or one of the prophets." He said to them, "But who do you say that I am?" Simon Peter said in reply, "You are the Messiah, the Son of the living God." Jesus said to him in reply, "Blessed are you, Simon son of Jonah. For flesh and blood* has not revealed this to you, but my heavenly Father. And so I say to you, you are Peter, and upon this rock I will build my church, and the gates of the netherworld shall not prevail against it. I will give you the keys to the kingdom of heaven. Whatever you bind on earth shall be bound in heaven; and whatever you loose on earth shall be loosed in heaven».
372. When they had finished breakfast, Jesus said to Simon Peter, "Simon, son of John, do you love me more than these?" He said to him, "Yes, Lord, you know that I love you." He said to him, "Feed my lambs." He then said to him a second time, "Simon, son of John, do you love me?" He said to him, "Yes, Lord, you know that I love you." He said to him, "Tend my sheep." He said to him the third time, "Simon, son of John, do you love me?" Peter was distressed that he had said to him a third time, "Do you love me?" and he said to him, "Lord, you know everything; you know that I love you." [Jesus] said to him, "Feed my sheep".

of reverence and obedience"[373]. In the last conclaves, the cardinals' collaborators and security guards who guarded the conclave outside the Sistine also entered for this greeting.

The ceremony ends with the recitation of the "Te Deum", the prayer with which the Church gives thanks to God.

At what point is the election and the name of the new Pontiff announced to the people?

Once the personal greeting of the cardinals is finished, the identity and the new name of the pope can be revealed to the world. It is the traditional "Habemus Papam!" "We have a pope!".

How much time elapses between the white smoke and the "Habemus Papam"?

Less than an hour elapses between the white smoke and the "Habemus Papam!".

Who announces the name of the new pope?

The person responsible for announcing the election of the new pope is the cardinal protodeacon (the senior Cardinal Deacon)[374]. He does so from the central balcony of St. Peter's Basilica, pronouncing these words:

373. Cfr. Ordo Rituum Conclavis, Year 2000, n. 71.
374. Cfr. Apostolic Constitution Universi Dominici Gregis (February 22, 1996) n. 89.

"Annuntio vobis gaudium magnum: habemus papam! Eminentissimum ac reverendissimum Dominum, Dominum (pronounces his first name), *Sanctae Romanae Ecclesiae Cardinalem* (pronounces the surname of the elected cardinal). *Qui sibi Nomen imposuit* (announces the name he will have as pope)*"*[375].

This is the translation:

"I announce to you a great joy: we have a pope. It is His Eminence and Reverence, Mr. (First name of the Cardinal elected) *Cardinal of the Holy Roman Church* (Surname of the Cardinal) *who has been given the name of* (Name of the new pontiff)*".*

Moments later, the new pope appears for the first time on the balcony of the basilica and makes his first speech, which is usually a brief greeting.

Who should accompany the pope on the balcony of St. Peter's Basilica?

Theoretically, he should be accompanied by the three cardinals who preside over each of the orders of bishops, priests and deacons[376].

What does the Pope do in his first public appearance?

After being officially introduced, he should impart the Apostolic "Urbi et Orbi" Blessing from the balcony of the Vatican Basilica[377]. If he wishes, he may give

375. Cfr. Ordo Rituum Conclavis, Year 2000, n. 74.
376. Cfr. "Sede Apostolica Vacante. Storia - Legislazione - Riti - Luoghi e cose". Ufficio delle Celebrazioni Liturgiche del Sommo Pontefice. Vatican City, 2005, p. 152.
377. Cfr. Apostolic Constitution Universi Dominici Gregis (February 22, 1996) n. 89.

a brief greeting.

What is the "Urbi et orbi" blessing?

The "Urbi et orbi" (to the city of Rome and to the world) blessing is a special blessing that can only be given by the Popes, and is reserved for the day of their election, Easter Sunday and the feast of Christmas. They can also decide to impart it in other very extraordinary circumstances of special need[378]. This blessing carries with it some particular indulgences for the faithful who desire them, and who receive it under the specific conditions requested by the Church: rejection of sin, sacramental confession, communion on the days immediately following, and finally, prayer for the pope.

When does the conclave conclude?

"The Conclave ends immediately after the new Supreme Pontiff assents to his election, unless he should determine otherwise"[379]. From that moment on, the electors can communicate with persons outside the Vatican.

What will be the first decisions of the new pope?

Among the first decisions will be to set the date for the Mass at the beginning of the pontificate, and to renew or replace the top officials of the Vatican Curia,

378. Pope Francis imparted an Urbi et Orbi blessing on March 27, 2020 at the height of the Covid-19 pandemic.
379. Cfr. Apostolic Constitution Universi Dominici Gregis (February 22, 1996) n. 91.

in particular the Secretary of State and the Prefects of the Dicasteries.

What should be the first ceremonies of the new pope?

It is customary that the day after his election the new pope celebrates Mass in the Sistine Chapel with all the cardinal electors and meets with them in the Sala Clementina of the Apostolic Palace.

In addition, a few days later will be the solemn ceremony of inauguration of the pontificate. He will wait about a week to allow the participation of representatives of the States and pilgrims. The Vatican law asks the pope to "within an appropriate time" also take possession of the Basilica of St. John Lateran, "according to the prescribed ritual"[380]. The main reason is that it is the cathedral of Rome.

When will the Mass for the beginning of the pontificate be?

In the past, it took place on the first Sunday or the first feast of precept after the election. That link no longer exists. It is usually celebrated no later than one week after his election. That date counts as the official day of the beginning of the pontificate, although technically he is pope from the very moment he accepts.

380. Cfr. Apostolic Constitution Universi Dominici Gregis (February 22, 1996) n. 92.

Can the cardinals reveal the secrets and details of the election once the conclave is over?

No, they cannot do so without specific permission from the pope. The law of the conclave states that "Cardinal electors are forbidden to reveal to any other person, directly or indirectly, information about the voting and about matters discussed or decided concerning the election of the Pope in the meetings of Cardinals, both before and during the time of the election"[381]. In fact, also the non-electing cardinals who participated in the previous meetings must keep secret what happens in those meetings[382].

Likewise, the norms order, "under grave weight of conscience", - the Latin expression 'graviter onerata ipsorum conscientia' is used -, "to maintain secrecy concerning these matters also after the election of the new Pope has taken place, and I remind them that it is not licit to break the secret in any way unless a special and explicit permission has been granted by the Pope himself"[383].

Has the secret of what happened during the conclave ever been revealed?

On occasion, secondary elements of the election have been leaked, which do not harm the freedom of either the elected pope or the cardinals who voted for him or did not vote for him.

In 2024, Pope Francis narrated in the book "The Successor" many unpublished details about the conclaves of April 2005 and March 2013[384]. As pope, he

381. Cfr. Apostolic Constitution Universi Dominici Gregis (February 22, 1996) n. 59.
382. Ibid.
383. Cfr. Apostolic Constitution Universi Dominici Gregis (February 22, 1996) n. 60.

can do so without violating secrecy.

Is an official record of the results of the vote tallies made?

The law of the conclave, the "Universi Dominici Gregis", establishes that once the conclave is concluded, the cardinal Camerlengo will leave written the result of the votes of each session, and that the text must be approved by the three cardinals in attendance. The document will be delivered to the new pope and "will be kept in a designated archive, enclosed in a sealed envelope, which may be opened by no one unless the Supreme Pontiff gives explicit permission"[385].

How will the voting record be kept, so as to ensure that secrecy is not violated?

The law of the conclave explains that the result of the voting at each session will be kept " in a designated archive, enclosed in a sealed envelope, which may be opened by no one unless the Supreme Pontiff gives explicit permission"[386]. It refers to a special section of the "Vatican Apostolic Archives", designated for "Reserved and Secret Documents", where "documents which, by their nature, are confidential and secret" are kept, which therefore "are excluded from consultation, even when the closed period is opened"[387], that is, the period relative to the pontiff who was elected in that conclave.

384. Cfr. "The Successor. My memories of Benedict XVI". Pope Francis and Javier Martínez-Brocal. Barcelona, Editorial Planeta (2024).
385. Cfr. Apostolic Constitution Universi Dominici Gregis (February 22, 1996) n. 60.
386. Ibid.
387. Cfr. Law on the Archives of the Holy See (March 21, 2005). Art. 39.

Do the conclave norms issued by John Paul II abrogate the norms of previous popes?

As is customary for the pope's norms, when they regulate a specific area, they repeal all the provisions that existed on that subject up to that date[388].

388. Cfr. Apostolic Constitution Universi Dominici Gregis (February 22, 1996) Promulgation.

Scandals

Is the Church holy?

In the prayer of the Creed it is declared that the Church is "holy", but this does not mean that those who form it, priests and laity, are good, perfect and pure - that would be pride and a lie. Although there are many valuable elements and many exemplary lives among the baptized, no one can deny that the seven deadly sins continue to be committed and that scandal and bad example are caused from within the Church. Jesus already warned about this, with the parable of the wheat and the tares[389].

On the other hand, from a faith perspective, although the Church is made up of sinful men and women, subject to every temptation and misery, at the same time they want to follow Christ and be part of the community founded by Him, and they receive the grace of the Holy Spirit that sanctifies God's work. Christians acknowledge their sins in the sacrament of the Mass and implore God's forgiveness in confession: but, at the same time, they recognize that God has the power to transform people as He has done with the saints.

In a theological sense, the holiness of the Church is

389. Matthew 13:24-30 and 36-43.

the constant and permanent effect of the redemptive work of Christ and of the action of the Holy Spirit present in the Church since the day of Pentecost.

Can a pope break celibacy or cause scandal?

Although it is not the most desirable thing to do, priests, bishops, cardinals and pontiffs, like any human being, are subject to all weaknesses and temptations. For this reason they pray and ask to be prayed for, to overcome victoriously every trial.

The sin of scandal is an immoral action that consists of giving bad example, inducing or inviting others to do evil. It is especially serious when committed against children. It is a bad conduct that causes others to turn away from God and the Church. Every Christian and, even more so, the ministers and the pope, are called to proclaim the Gospel, which means "*good news*". Scandal is the opposite of this, because it becomes bad newss.

Can an ecclesiastic lead a double life and, for example, steal, prevaricate or have sexual relations?

The Church asks of its ministers a life of honesty and congruence with the values of the Gospel. Therefore, it does not permit that those who lead it live a double life. In the case of celibacy, required of priests of the Latin rite, the Church assumes that the priest renounces maintaining sentimental relationships. If he does not do so, he is acting gravely against his commitment and against the good of the Church. Just as a husband acts scandalously against his wife when he has relations with another woman, breaking his promise of fidelity, so also the priest who would have a relationship would be affecting not only himself, but also the person with whom he maintains such a relationship and the Church itself.

The Code of Canon Law provides for severe penalties for those who act in this manner and may remove the offender from ministry. In addition, it prohibits, under penalty of excommunication, the priest in question from absolving his accomplice in crimes in these matters. On the other hand, trusting in the right intention of the ministers and the pursuit of a right conscience, the Church authorities cannot behave like detectives without just cause. It would be as if a wife were spying on her husband all the time to be sure that he is faithful to her.

Why did it take so long for child abuse cases to come to public light?

There are many sides to this sensitive issue. Pope Francis thanked journalists for what they did to bring these terrible crimes to light. *"I thank you for what you tell us about what is wrong in the Church, for how much you help us not to sweep it under the carpet and for the voice you have given to the victims of abuse, thank you for that"*[390].

Experience shows that people who have been abused need a long time, often many years, to tell what happened and to denounce the culprits. They often prefer to remain silent for fear of not being believed, of reopening the wound, or because the person who abused them is someone close to them (a relative, a family friend, a priest dear to them). These situations were considered so shameful for those who

390. Imposition of the insignia of Knight and Dame of the Grand Cross of the Order of the Piano on Philip Pullella and Valentina Alazraki. November 13, 2021.

suffered from them that they preferred that no one knew about them.

On the other hand, in the past the word of children was not given the value it is given today and the voice of adults was privileged. In part, this meant that what the victims said was discredited by their own parents or adult relatives.

Another serious reason was the excess of confidence on the part of the ecclesiastical authority and the faithful, towards those whom society had always considered blameless, such as priests or community leaders.

Fortunately, sensitivity has changed and the victims of any crime have learned from such unfortunate cases to report immediately; adults pay more attention to the word of children and the law defends their rights; the ecclesiastical authority and society, although to the unjust detriment of some, has demystified the figure of priests and has learned to see them as people with strengths and weaknesses. Above all, it is no longer cause for shame to denounce being victims of aggression or crime.

Did all the cases of pederasty reach the Vatican?

In 2001, Cardinal Joseph Ratzinger convinced John Paul II to require bishops to send abuse cases to the Vatican, so that the culprits could be tried directly there. The central problem was that dioceses, in many cases, were avoiding taking strong action against abusers, so Ratzinger decided to take personal charge of this drama.

Starting from that point, in general, the way of

proceeding was that the bishop should follow up on the denunciation and send it to the Vatican only if he was certain of the abuse. The point is that these are crimes that occur in secret and are not always easy to prove. In many cases, if there was no proof or the complaint was not ratified, the priest was not considered guilty and could continue to minister in the same or another parish. Thus, the naivety of some bishops and overconfidence in their priests led them to act unjustly, weighing their scales in favor of the accused and causing unfair treatment of the victims and in practice a certain degree of cover-up in the Church.

After being elected pope, Benedict XVI again tightened legislation to give greater weight to the victim and, in cases of justified suspicion, suspend the accused from ministry, proceed to trial and notify the Holy See. Benedict was also the first pontiff to meet with victims of abuse to personally offer his response as leader of the Church.

What have recent popes done to address abuse?

John Paul II undertook “Operation Clean Sweep” in 1993, with a letter with precise indications for U.S. bishops[191]. At the time, 20% of the dioceses did not give it any weight and stubbornly continued to cover up these cases and the culprits. In 2001, at the request of Cardinal Joseph Ratzinger, John Paul II requested that all cases be sent to the Vatican to ensure that the abusers were prosecuted. Until then they were judged either in their dioceses or by the Congregation for the Clergy. Ratzinger ensured that the accused were not favored by local judges who were familiar with

391. Cfr. John Paul II. “Letter to the Bishops of the United States of America, June 11, 1993.

them, and that they received harsher penalties than had been the case until then. In 2002, the Polish pontiff had to raise his voice again to tell the bishops that "there is no place in the priesthood or religious life for those who harm young people"[392]. It was the norm of "zero tolerance".

In 2005, when Benedict XVI was elected pope, he made it a general rule to expel abusers from the priesthood. Thus, he expelled at least a hundred priests a year. He also decided to meet personally with the victims, to express his closeness and solidarity. He was the first pope to make such a gesture.

Francis went a step further. He decided that sanctions would not be limited to abuser priests, but also to bishops who had not acted forcefully in response to the allegations, since that in practice meant covering up for criminals. Thus, he dismissed at least a dozen prelates. Since March 2023, moreover, he began to call to account for cover-ups also lay people who have presided over Catholic institutions. Culturally, he proposed to get to the root of these events. He said that these crimes are committed when there is a climate of "elitism and clericalism" and that as a general rule they are "abuses of conscience, abuses of power and sexual abuse", a triple crime.

Another of his initiatives was to convene in February 2019 a summit of presidents of bishops' conferences to reinforce their sensitivity and protagonism in the pending tasks: help for victims, "cleaning house" of delinquent priests and prevention of abuse in all areas. He also established that bishops should investigate all cases that come to their attention; that each diocese should open a "stable and easily accessible" office where those who wish to do so can file com-

392. Cfr. John Paul II, Address at the meeting with U.S. Cardinals, April 23, 2002.

plaints; and that the gravity of the crime when the victim is an adult in a "vulnerable" situation should be equated to cases where the victim is a minor.

What repercussions have the news of abuse had inside and outside the Church?

The general reaction has been one of indignation, annoyance, embarrassment and disappointment. On the other hand, knowledge of the allegations has helped the Church to modify procedures and ways of acting. For example, in general, entry into the seminary is no longer allowed for those with the age of children or in early adolescence. Also, the profile of the formators of future priests is being better monitored and psychological help is being given to identify attitudes that impede the serene exercise of the ministry. Another change is that now the bishops must diligently attend to any complaint or denunciation that reaches them, either through the media or through the permanent offices in the diocese.

Unfortunately, many good priests are now viewed with suspicion. Some religious groups of other denominations have taken advantage of the scandal to invite Catholics to leave the Church and join them. There are reports of some, but not all, so-called victim assistance groups that have taken advantage of the situation to profit from it, seeking financial gain for their own benefit rather than providing comprehensive support.

What is the Church's legislation to punish and eliminate pederasty abuses?

In July 2010, the then Vatican spokesman Federico Lombardi, in an extensive note, gave a general outline of the norms in force in the Catholic Church for dealing with abuses, and reconstructed the evolution they had undergone in recent years. It was the first time that it was clearly exposed.

In 2001, John Paul II had promulgated the law "Sacramentorum sanctitatis tutela", with which he transferred the competence to treat and judge these crimes in the canonical sphere to the Congregation for the Doctrine of the Faith[393]. This decree was accompanied by "Norms of application and procedure", which had reference to a name in Latin, "Normae de gravioribus delictis", "Norms of the most serious crimes", for how this dicastery would deal with these processes. It referred to crimes against the sacraments of the Eucharist and Penance, but also to sexual abuse committed by a cleric with a person under 18 years of age.

In 2010, Benedict XVI updated these norms to make the procedures faster, and to make it possible in the most serious cases for the pope to sentence the offender to be expelled from the priesthood. He also modified the statute of limitations period for these crimes from ten to twenty years from the time the victim reaches the age of majority, and left the door open to the possibility of repeal beyond that period. He also reminded the bishops that it is important to collaborate with the civil authorities in these cases, and that, therefore, "the provisions of civil law regarding the reporting of offenses to the competent authorities must always be followed."

393. It is now called the Dicastery for the Doctrine of the Faith.

In 2023, Francis again tightened these rules. With the law "Vos estis lux mundi", "You are the light of the world", he established a complaint procedure against bishops who had committed abuse or who "by action or by omission" had covered up for alleged priests. The norm included the possibility of sanctioning lay leaders who were in charge of Church movements and who had not acted diligently when they received reports of abuse.

Francis also ordered that each diocese have a structure "stable and easily accessible to the public, so that they can present signs (of abuse)". He asked that priests and religious report there immediately any abuse of which they have "news or well-founded reasons for suspicion," except for those known by confession. When that office receives a complaint, it must inform the Vatican and investigate to decide whether to open a process or shelve it. Regardless of where the complaint was filed, the bishop of the place where the abuse occurred is responsible for this preliminary investigation.

The law also prohibited the imposition of any bonds of silence on whistleblowers or victims. This leaves them free to take civil legal action.

Is it not true that the Vatican too often employs secrecy?

All persons and institutions have the right to handle their data and information in accordance with legitimate interests. There are just reasons that may lead individuals or institutions not to disclose their private information. For example, when it concerns personal and intimate matters and does not need to be known by others; or ongoing investigations that, if published, could be hindered.

Naturally it can also refer to shameful matters. The Vatican, besides being a civil state, represents a religion that preaches honesty, truthfulness and charity. Therefore, in that case, if they are not published with the intention of covering them up, it would be a serious inconsistency.

In general, nations have a secret archive for their government affairs, which is only made public after a certain time or under special circumstances. This is the reason why the Vatican Archives, formerly called the Secret Archives, allows several decades to pass before opening to scholars the material related to a pontificate. Currently, all the documents of the Vatican and the papal secretariat up to 1958, when Pius XII died, are available for consultation.

Is it true that the book of Revelation prophesies the fall of the Vatican?

To correctly interpret biblical texts it is important to study their context and the time in which they were written, otherwise the interpretations tend to be partial and mistaken. Some religious groups who are enemies of the Catholic Church affirm that the destruction of the Church is prophesied in the Holy Scriptures. With this, they not only manifest their hatred and envy of the Church instituted by Christ, but also their dirty intentions, their lack of honesty and the way in which they manipulate the Word of God.

The book of Revelation was written by the Apostle John at a time when the Church was persecuted by the Roman Empire. Since the year 64, the emperor Nero had begun a cruel persecution against all Christians: all their property was taken from them and they were condemned to death. Except for St. John, all the apostles were martyred. He was exiled and suffered persecution, like many Christians, men and women of his time.

Some thought then that it was the end of the Church and that the power of the Empire would end up destroying what Christ had founded. Under these circumstances, God inspired St. John to write the book of Revelation. Its purpose was that the Christians of that and all ages would discover that, even in the midst of tribulations or persecutions, the power of God would always triumph.

John wrote this biblical text using many symbols, as did some Old Testament prophets, such as Daniel or Ezekiel. And just as in the Old Testament Babylon was referred to as "the great whore", because its king intended to destroy the people of Israel, John applied it to the power of the Roman Empire that intended to destroy the Church, the new people of God.

Understanding these symbolisms, the context of Revelation and its parallelism with the Old Testament, it is understood that when the apostle prophesies the fall of Rome and calls it "Babylon", "the Great Whore" or "the city of the seven hills", he points to how the Roman power of his time would fall defeated, while the Church would continue its mission throughout the centuries.

There is a great difference between the Rome that persecuted Christians and the Rome of today, the destination of millions of pilgrims who are proud to be Christians and come to venerate the remains of Peter, Paul and many martyrs. This city became the seat of the Pope, the successor of Peter and guide of the Church who, in prosperity and adversity, with calm and martyrdom, presides over the Church to lead it to Christ.

Those who try to use the text of Revelation to denigrate the Church should remember the words Christ said to Peter: " And so I say to you, you are Peter, and upon this rock I will build my church, and the gates of the netherworld shall not prevail against it"[394].

394. Mt 16:18

Jubilee

What are the Jubilees or Holy Years?

With the motive of special anniversaries of the Birth of Christ, popes convoke "Jubilees". These are periods during which pilgrims travel to Rome and pray at the tomb of the apostle Peter to receive spiritual graces.

The idea is to underline how this historical fact continues to have profound consequences for humanity. Thus, the Jubilee is an invitation to meditate on the meaning of this fact in one's own life, to consider it from the perspective of the Christian message and to make the resolution to strive against the evil that each one personally commits.

A concrete practice of the Jubilee is to pass through the "Holy Door" in St. Peter's Basilica and in the other papal basilicas of Rome, as a gesture of the decision to ask God's help to start again with the purpose of doing good and avoiding evil.

What is the Holy Door?

This is the name given to a door of the papal basilicas that ordinarily remains closed and is opened only during the "Holy Years" or Jubilees. It is opened by the pope with a ceremony in which he invites the faithful to live a time of seeking God's grace and of repentance for one's sins. Passing through this door evokes the willingness to change one's life and to receive God's mercy. For this reason, those who do so by fulfilling the established requirements (repudiation of sin, even venial sin, going to confession, receiving communion and praying for the pope's intentions) obtain a plenary indulgence.

What is plenary indulgence?

An indulgence is a special grace of the Catholic Church, which cancels in the soul of the person who receives it the punishment he or she has deserved for the sins for which he or she has previously confessed and received absolution.

Who was the first pope to open a Holy Door?

The first pontiff to open a Holy Door was Alexander VI, in the year 1500. It was the seventh Jubilee or Holy Year of the Catholic Church. On that occasion he opened the Holy Door in the basilicas of St. Peter's, St. Paul's Outside the Walls and St. Mary Major.

How often is there a Jubilee or Holy Year?

The first Jubilee of the Catholic Church was convoked in the year 1300 by Pope Boniface VIII. From then on, pilgrimages to Rome and visits to the tombs of the apostles Peter and Paul became very popular.

Initially the idea was to celebrate the Jubilee every 100 years, but in 1350 a new one was called and it was established that it would be every 50 years, so that each new generation could participate in one. Later, it was thought that it should be every 33 years, to commemorate the anniversary of the Resurrection of Christ, but in the end this idea did not come to fruition.

In 1475 the Jubilee was renamed "Holy Year" and since then it has been celebrated every 25 years.

The Jubilee of 1500 was the first to include the rite of the opening of the Holy Door in each of the four major basilicas of Rome. Since then, this has been one of the most important events of each Holy Year.

In 1933 a special Jubilee was celebrated to commemorate the "Year of the Redemption", the 1900 years of the Resurrection of Christ, without ceasing to convoke Jubilees every 25 years.

Paul VI celebrated the Jubilee in 1975.

In 1983 Pope John Paul II decided to celebrate an Extraordinary Holy Year also for the 1950th anniversary of the Resurrection of Jesus and in preparation for the Holy Year 2000.

In 2015, Francis convoked the "Jubilee of Mercy", which was celebrated from December 8, 2015 to November 20, 2016. Symbolically, he inaugurated it with the opening of the Holy Door in the Cathedral of Bangui (Central African Republic) and not in St. Peter's Basilica.

The 2025 Jubilee was entitled "Pilgrims of Hope".

Made in the USA
Coppell, TX
22 April 2025

48590956R00167